BORIS JOHNSON

MEDIA CREATION

MEDIA CLOWN

MEDIA CASUALTY?

Edited by
John Mair
with
Andrew Beck
and
Paul Connew

CONTENTS

Acknowledgements

Curated books are sums of their parts. Especially when published against the clock. Writers have to be commissioned, cajoled, and edited before publication. These books have breakneck schedules. I am writing this just four weeks after Boris Johnson resigned as Conservative party leader. A new leader and Prime Minister is imminent. The writing has been quick and very often simply superb. I thank all the contributors for their work and their patience in the face of my email harassment. They are the stars of this volume.

Andrew Beck and Paul Connew were my fellow editors, with me right from the start of this project. Andrew copy-edited the book, and liaised with contributors. Paul also liaised with contributors, and was often asked to produce copy at very short notice and under difficult circumstances. I thank them very much. Simply not possible without them.

I am also grateful to Dean Stockton for an, as ever, brilliant cover; Roger Packer for his publishing skills; and to my (still, just) as ever patient wife Susan Ann who confined me to the dining table during lockdown. Still there and still creating volume after volume.

John Mair, Oxford, 4 August 2022

About the Editors

John Mair is the most prolific editor/author on matters journalistic in Britain. This is his 49th 'hackademic' book mixing hacks and academics in short order. He helped to invent the genre. Subjects have ranged from the Leveson Report to the future of the BBC to the pandemic to more recently the Oxford of Inspector Morse and the huge oil boom in his native land-Guyana – 'Oil Dorado'. John was a BBC (and other broad-casters) producer and a teacher of journalism in previous lives. He lives in Oxford.

Andrew Beck is author of best-selling and oft-cited works such as Cultural Work and Communication Studies: The Essential Introduction. He is a former teacher and educational manager, chief examiner for public and professional examinations, and continues to research and publish on a range of media issues.

Paul Connew is a media commentator and broadcaster, former editor of the Sunday Mirror, deputy editor of the Daily Mirror, and US Mirror Group bureau chief. He writes and broadcasts frequently on media and political issues in the UK and abroad.

By way of a general introduction

He was a slow(ish) burn on the way to being 'World King'/Prime Minister. Lusting after the role from a child, he lasted barely three years in the job before his party and his lying brought him down.

One Thursday in July 2022 he was hob-nobbing with world leaders at a Nato summit in Spain, having come with many of them from a G7 Summit in Germany and before that a Commonwealth Heads of Government Meeting in Rwanda. The next Thursday he was delivering, rather ungraciously, his resignation speech as party leader/Prime Minister from a swiftly erected lectern in Downing Street.

In his own words that day, 'dems the breaks'. The wrong way in his case. His dream had ended. The sad comic opera that was the Johnson premiership is the narrative thread of this collection. Will he now shuffle off stage? Read on and you decide.

OVERTURE AND BEGINNERS

Postcode powerplay: Where does Boris Johnson belong?

Peter York argues that if you want to identify the original Boris Johnson from amongst competing accounts, you should turn to geo-demographics: postcodes

Who do we think Boris Johnson is? There are three partial answers. The first is comedy-toff: a bit like the late comic actor Terry Thomas. Toff-U-Like. An amusing him-off from the telly.

The second is that he's a certain kind of Tory. But which kind exactly? He says he's the 'One Nation' kind, the benign patrician kind. He's got the style. But notable One Nation Tories tend to disagree. This doesn't matter because the One Nation Tories are completely out in the modern Conservative party!

Finally, if you're a bit modern and deep and favour individual psychology, you could think of him as a personality type. His American counterpart Donald Trump has been constantly identified as having narcissistic personality disorder. Mr Johnson famously said at four that he wanted to be 'world king'. So what does that make him?

Welcome to my world

I'm a market researcher by background, and way back in 1978 research nerds got a marvellous new tool to help them understand groups of people; it was called geo-demographics (GDs). The premise of GDs is that you are where you live. It meant that if you wanted to know a lot about a group of people who were important to you – customers, supporters, voters – you only needed an address list. An outfit called ACORN (A Classification Of Residential Neighbourhoods) put an enormous amount of computing power behind a data bank of knowledge about the postcode building blocks of residential areas, material originally derived from the National Census. Birds of a feather flock together was the thinking. It's all been redeveloped with new cleverer data inputs since then, but that remains the big idea.

Despite the distraction of his exotic bloodlines revealed in the BBC's Who Do You Think You Are in 2008 – Turkish, French, German, Jewish, royal – his family's Devon farm, his US birthplace, and cosmopolitan Euro-stints, the adult Mr Johnson is most consistently a Londoner. What can we tell about him from the kind of Londoner he's been? What do Mr Johnson's London milieux and his postcodes say about him?

Judge Boris by his address

I know a fair few of those places and the people who live in them, and I think I know what they mean. I'd say the Johnson-world London geography and milieux could identify him as precisely the social type populist Tories and Johnson-loving newspapers like The Mail and Express say they really loathe. Judged by his postcodes, Boris Johnson is that hate figure of right-wing populist propagandists the world over – a member of 'The Metropolitan Liberal Elite'.

(It's worth saying here that some unkind people say that Mr Johnson is a natural loner and hasn't got any real friends, so you can't argue from the milieux. But his constant biographer Andrew Gimson says this simply isn't true and there are lots of close long-time friends and named some to me.)

Just consider for one sparkling moment how many of Johnson's London postcodes have had an N in them. Primrose Hill (NW1) and Islington (N1) for instance are Daily Mail code for 'not like us', meaning comfortably-off people who have talkative dinner parties where pretentious foodie talk is interwoven with identity politics – what the Boris-loving papers call 'Woke-ism' now.

At these parties, so the tabloid story goes, everyone is constantly doing 'virtue-signalling', the Spectator phrase for parading fashionable liberal sentiments. It's an updated, clever, way of saying hypocrite. Mr Johnson's lived around these people and these places for decades, the places where better-paid newspaper hacks and TV people live, people who are socially liberal even if they're dry on the economy.

Besides Boris Johnson and his close 'liberal' family connections, his maternal grandfather Sir James Fawcett, a distinguished barrister, was for twenty years a member of the ECHR (the European Commission for Human Rights), the body that the Johnson Government has decided to ignore. And for nine years of it its President. And Mr Johnson's sister Rachel Johnson famously said of her father that he had a habit of marrying 'leftie' women. Boris's second wife Marina, daughter of the BBC correspondent Charles Wheeler, is widely regarded as an Islington leftie.

No N in SWI or 3

Now these N places are decidedly nice, but they're not where the hyper-toffs and the plutocrats live. They're absolutely not like Knightsbridge (SW1X), Belgravia (SW1), Mayfair (W1), Heavy Kensington (W8), or Chelsea (SW3), the areas where the Masters of the Universe live when they're in London. That's where hedge-fund kings and Goldman grandees live, or Lords with London estates (Grosvenor, Cadogan, Portman, De Walden, Phillimore). People with eponymous 'global companies', or non-dom billionaire newspaper proprietors. People vastly richer than those nice N people. People so rich they can afford to give hundreds of thousands – even millions – to political parties.

These are people today's Tory MPs have to take very seriously. On 6 June 2022, Nadine Dorries, the DCMS Secretary of State, told a Sky News interviewer in the Central Lobby that Johnson's Tory critics should wake up and realise that the party's biggest donors wanted Boris as leader whatever happened. So there. Grow up.

Where the liberal luvvies are

Over time, a number of the Metropolitan Liberal Elite have had to suck up to those Global Masters if they wanted power. Tony Blair, who used to live in a rather similar house (in Richmond Crescent N1 0LZ) to Johnson's former marital Islington home (a tall, thin Georgian terrace of course N1 8AP) a decade before, had to do it with Rupert Murdoch. Now he's got some Serious Money, Blair lives in a W1 garden square and in Sir John Gielgud's old house in the country.

The stereotype of the Metropolitan Liberal Elite is intended to make people well outside the capital think that well-paid liberal luvvies actually run the world. That a few writers, TV presenters, directors and those leftie comedians who can fill big halls, are in charge. But really being in charge now needs a combination of professional skills – digital media, PR, lobbying, all the American 'political technology' things Dominic

Cummings was constantly on about – employed by people who turn up at the office at 8am and never stop, and funded with money from big donors, people for whom a spare couple of million is 'No Problem'.

Is Boris really an N person?

Despite being an N person with N person money – Boris Johnson appears convinced he has no money and constantly faces imminent ruin – he's unusually well-connected with people who are vastly grander and richer than him. In part it's Eton – most of these N people went to lesser public schools – and partly because he's been a celebrity for more than two decades. Toffs and plutocrats like famous faces at their parties. And even more when they've got political potential too.

If you want to be world king, you've got to know people who'd give your neighbours in N1 8AP the vapours. And you've got to learn from people like Cummings. Or even from Trump's campaign manager Steve Bannon, who notably claimed in an American documentary (The Brink) that he'd co-written Mr Johnson's 2018 resignation speech as Foreign Secretary from Theresa May's Cabinet. Andrew Gimson says Bannon is a wild exaggerator and that Johnson, with British self-deprecating charm, would've let him think he'd contributed a lot, but then written what he'd intended in the first place.

Matthew D'Ancona doesn't agree, he sees the links between Johnson and Bannon as very significant. At the same time, 'the matter of his relationship with President Trump's former chief strategist is almost uniquely sensitive, and Johnson hates being asked about it by journalists'. Which is possibly why the BBC and many mainstream journalists have avoided asking Mr Johnson about it. He clearly doesn't think it's a good look.

Which postcode next for Boris?

In summer 2022 some of those Big Money people, people like Lord Cruddas (recently elevated by Mr Johnson and allegedly worth £1.321bn) claimed that there'd been a coup against Boris Johnson and he should be restored to power by putting him on the Conservative Party members' ballot. And their eager booster Nadine Dorries – widely tipped for a peerage in Johnson's final 'Honours' list – has described the process as 'a coup' too. Does she mean illegal and therefore a reversal could be legitimate?

If this stirs worries in N1 then wise heads say it could never happen here, that Brits would never rally round a Big Steal story like the one still believed by 61 per cent of 2020 Trump voters, even after the revelations from the January 6 Committee hearings. No gent of any kind, no One Nation Tory and certainly no one who'd ever lived in N1.

References

Clive Hammond (2020) 'Boris Johnson's 'dream to be world King' unearthed as he rips apart Downing Street', The Express, 16 November, www.express.co.uk/news/uk/1360622/boris-johnson-news-brexit-latest-eu-trade-talks-conservative-party-downing-street-spt
YouTube (2022) 'Nadine Dorries blames 'Remainers' for confidence vote', Sky News, 6 June 2022
www.youtube.com/watch?v=ZMm9LWHxjmc 2:39
Carole Cadwalladr (2019) 'Video reveals Steve Bannon links to Boris Johnson', The Guardian, 22 June
www.theguardian.com/us-news/2019/jun/22/video-reveals-steve-bannon-links-to-boris-johnson
Matthew D'Ancona (2019) 'Bannon's Britain', Tortoise Media
28 September 2019,
members.tortoisemedia.com/2019/09/28/bannons-britain/content.html

About the contributor

Peter York is a 'capitalist tool' by background, as a market researcher and management consultant. In parallel he is a social commentator, journalist, occasional TV presenter, and author of eleven books, ranging from the best-selling Official Sloane Ranger Handbook to Authenticity is a Con, an attack on the cult of authenticity. His latest book, co-written with Professor Patrick Barwise, is The War Against the BBC (Penguin 2020). He is the President of The Media Society.

ACT ONE:
BORIS THE JOURNALIST

Early days, early ways

**Boris Johnson has been a journalist/politician
(not always in that order) for all his working life.
John Mair's delving into his early 'professional'
days in London and Brussels yields some
interesting results on the Boris Johnson
modus operandi – lying – which eventually
led to his downfall as Prime Minister**

Boris Johnson is a hack in the worst sense of the word. Outside of journalism he has only had one 'proper' job: a wannabe management consultant straight after Oxford Classics. He resigned after a week. From then to now he's been a journalist or journalist politician. This is his metier, usually getting jobs through connections and simple nepotism and a modicum of writing talent.

This chapter relies heavily on two of Boris' (anti) Boswells – Tom Bower and his book Boris Johnson The Gambler (2020) and Sonia Purnell's Just Boris: The Irresistible Rise of a Political Celebrity (2011). Both are thick and well researched tomes on the Bojo phenomenon, and both cracking reads.

After Classics at Oxford and a near disaster of being close to being thrown off the course for laziness (a story yet to be told), he got an Upper Second which has always rankled with him, it was The Thunderer for him in 1987 when The Times was still in its prime. Connections worked to get him into Wapping. He was farmed out to the Wolverhampton Express and Star to learn journalism. The Black Country was not Boris' natural territory. In his news editor Derek Turner's view he 'would never make it as a reporter'. London was not much easier. One of his mentors on the paper, David Sapsted, recalls how Boris was recalled from a job in Dover reporting a seamen's strike as 'he can't cope'.

First sacking

Back to base at The Times where he was put on grunt work rewriting agency and other copy and rarely allowed out. But he hit his first career disaster in 1988 in a 'story' about Edward II and his boy lover – a catamite – Piers Gaveston. Boris has always been good at using language. It included a 'quote' from a Classics don at Balliol College, Colin Lucas, who was also Boris' godfather. Trouble is that it was quite simply made up and historically inaccurate. Dr Lucas complained to the then Editor of The Times, a rough Scot Charlie 'Gorbals' Wilson. Wilson was no lover of toffs, even faux toffs. Boris was dragged into his office and carpeted. He repeated the error and magnified it in a 'clarification' story four days later. This time Boris was told by Wilson his crime was 'heinous', yet he pleaded that all quotes in The Times were made up. He was sacked, out on his ear.

Saved by the Daily Telegraph

Max Hastings, the then-editor of the Daily Telegraph, had encountered Boris at the Oxford Union and been impressed. Their mutual contact Miriam Gross reconnected them. Hastings liked mavericks and hired him in 1989. Later he was to have much buyer's remorse and become one of Johnson the politician's harshest critics.

Boris made an impression, not always a positive one, on this paper. Talking over others in editorial conferences did not impress colleagues. Once again it was the gruel of minor stories and rewrites for young Boris. Then in 1989 Hastings had the idea of causing mischief by sending Boris to be a Brussels correspondent with the brief to debunk the EC. For five years that was the Boris schtick and how he made his name in journalism. Big story after big story splashed into the Telegraph from Brussels. Many were sensational, only some were true or partly true. Boris' reputation there was based on lies or exaggerations, not for the first or, indeed, for the last time.

Getting Brexit on the media agenda

Boris' own private views were pro-European. After all he had been brought up in Brussels with Stanley, a Eurocrat father, and went to school there. Publicly though he was the Berlaymont basher in chief. In many ways his 'journalism' there laid the foundations for Ukip and the Brexit vote. His fellow national newspaper hacks there had been a cosy cartel. They treated him with great suspicion. Some, like Geoff Meade, tried to initiate and help him. As ever, Boris accepted their help then bit off the hand that had fed him, the habit of a lifetime.

His style was unique: late for press conferences, dishevelled (though the blond hair had not yet been ruffled for effect), standing at the back taking no notes. His job was to be a provocateur to the bureaucrats. The 'true' anti-EC stories tumbled out: 'curved bananas were to be banned', 'Italy fails to measure up on condoms', 'Brussels recruits sniffers to ensure that Euro-manure smells the same', 'first EC cheese row takes the biscuit', 'fishermen made to wear hair nets', and 'Berlaymont to be blown up after asbestos found'. You name an idiocy and Boris 'reported' it.

That lack of notebook in press conferences meant Boris could simply make up quotes to fit his stories and prejudices. His professional voice was firmly that of the 'Up yours Delors' Eurosceptic tendency.

Dirtying the UK/EC pond

Boris was in Brussels at a crunch point it EU/UK relations. PM Margaret Thatcher was hand-bagged at the Rome Summit in 1990. Her successor John Major tried to balance the demands of membership with the increasingly vocal Tory Eurosceptic right. Not always well. Hence the vote of confidence he called in 1993.

Boris became a firm thorn in the side of both the Berlaymont bureaucrats and the Tory Europhile ministers. Foreign Secretary Douglas Hurd was said to have 'had words' with his editor. Both denied it. Hurd's Foreign Office set up a rapid rebuttal unit to counter Boris and other Eurosceptic journalists like Christopher Booker. Later, PM John Major actually (negatively) namechecked Boris at an end of summit press conference in 1991 for his 'grenades'.

Do they mean him?

What did his fellow hacks think of Boris the bright star journalist? They spent five years playing catch-up, being cajoled by their news desk into following up Johnson's 'stories'. Here are their comments, nearly all negative, some anonymous.

David Usborne of The Times: 'He wasn't making things up necessarily, just overegging to a degree that was dishonest. I always assumed he didn't believe that stuff'.

James Landale, then of The Times, later of the BBC: 'Boris told such dreadful lies. It made one gasp and stretch one's eyes'.

Anonymous broadcaster in Brussels: 'He gets away with murder because he is charming'.

Sarah Helm of The Independent: 'A complete charlatan'.

Sonia Purnell, his boss at the Telegraph Brussels Bureau: 'His bluster and wit serves to obscure his real politics, which are nasty. He is a charmingly evasive and ruthless customer'.

Anonymous fellow writer: 'As a reporter he was shite. As a writer of intellectual ability, of course, he became something else'.

John Palmer of The Guardian remembers Johnson lifting his research on a Delors EU plan and turning it round to suit his agenda: 'as a journalist he is thoroughly irresponsible. Inventing stories' is his judgement.

Adieu Brussels, hello again London

Yet, despite their professional reservations, the press corps gave him a standing ovation on his last day. The EU spokesman thanked him through gritted teeth.

James Landale: 'Boris had become such a pariah amongst the EU officials that no one would talk to him anymore. He was by then a caricature figure and he had to go'.

Geoff Meade of the Press Association (an early Brussels mentor): 'When Boris was here it was a golden era. We will never see his likes again'.

Boris, as ever, saw it in a different light. On Desert Island Discs to Sue Lawley in 2005: 'I was chucking these rocks over the garden wall and I listened to this amazing crash from the greenhouse next door.'

Sacked again, nearly

In 1990 he was nearly sacked a second time. It came to light that he had offered to have beaten up a fellow journalist who was investigating his old Etonian pal Darius Guppy. Guppy was later jailed for insurance fraud. There was a tape. Max Hastings dragged him to London for a carpeting. Boris talked his way out this time. But the tape later became public and Boris was hijacked with it by Ian Hislop on Have I Got News For You in 1998. Boris' gaffes then and now always get him in the end.

Hastings is coruscating in his epitaph: '[F]irst, he will say absolutely anything to man, woman or child that will give them pleasure at that moment, heedless of whether he may be obliged to contradict it ten minutes later. Second, having registered his wild-card status as a brand, he exploits it to secure absolution for a procession of follies, gaffes, idiocies and scoundrelisms, such as would destroy the career of any other man or woman in journalism, never mind government.'

So, much talent, much enterprise, many lies. A useful summary of the life of Boris Johnson the journalist and the politician.

References

Tom Bower (2020) Boris Johnson The Gambler, London: WH Allen.
Sonia Purnell (2011) Just Boris: The Irresistible Rise Of A Political Celebrity, London: Aurum Press.

The end of the affair

For 12 years Tim Walker was a colleague of Boris Johnson on The Daily Telegraph. He saw how the future prime minister dragged the newspaper – and almost the entire industry – down to his level

One of the greatest and most enduring love affairs of my life is in its death throes, and, not for the first time, it's Boris Johnson who's the third party and principally to blame. There have been letters, and, just lately, a telephone call, and, quite frankly, I'm devastated.

In the 30 years we've been together, I don't believe I've changed at all, but the newspaper industry has, beyond recognition. Cynicism as well as idealism has always been there, of course, but Johnson more or less single-handedly drained it of the latter. He blurred the distinction between news and comment, the journalists who report on politicians and the politicians, and, all of a sudden, individuals who genuinely ventured into the trade to do good are finding themselves actively engaged in doing bad. They've lost sight of the best interests of their readers – standing up for the little guy against the big guy – and concern themselves only, as Johnson used to, with the best interests of their non-dom owners.

A gun for sale

Johnson's ignoble career in newspapers has been well documented, but less well understood is how he's poisoned the well of journalism every bit as much as he has the political one. Sacked by The Times for lying, he then washed up at the Telegraph, where he was quick to see there was a good living to be had out of lying about the European Union, first for Lord Conrad Black, and then, after they acquired the title from the Europhobic fraudster, the non-dom billionaire knights, David and Frederick Barclay. Words became Johnson's soldiers in a vicious ground war against anyone and any institution that stood in his way and the grim Darwinian alt-right vision of his owners who paid him £270,000 a year.

I remember my first sight of Johnson at an editorial conference at the Telegraph and the revulsion was instant. He was very obviously in the business of confirming prejudices rather than challenging them: he'd make lazy, clichéd jokes about foreigners, minority groups, the working classes, Liverpudlians, and women he claimed to have bedded. He was the Barclays' man through and through, and made little or no attempt at small talk with the likes of me. He saw no need to expend energy on endearing himself to factory floor journalists when he had the owners on his side.

The power and the glory

Talk to any journalist of my generation about why they wanted to get into the business and the chances are All The President's Men will come up, and this brings me to the telephone call I received. That film about how The Washington Post had broken Watergate and brought down President Nixon had made the industry seem noble and glamorous. Fifty years on almost to the day from the start of the Post's famous investigation, one of its journalists called me and made me profoundly depressed. It brought home to me quite how far newspapers in this country had fallen and what a chasm had opened up between my youthful ideals and the present reality.

She was doing a piece about Carriegate. This was a very different kind of 'gate' from the one the Post had broken. I'd disclosed in The New European how The Times had run a story about Johnson as Foreign Secretary improperly attempting to secure a £100,000-a-year job for his then-mistress Carrie Symonds. It made the first edition of The Times, but then it had been mysteriously pulled from all the subsequent ones. The Mail's website, which had first lifted it, then swiftly took it down.

The Ministry of Fear

The official explanation I got from the most senior people at The Times was that the Johnsons had threatened legal action. Given that the story has since been endlessly repeated and no one has been sued, that just beggars belief. Simon Walters, the freelance journalist whose byline appeared on the original story, assured me he stood by it 100 per cent and he added he could stand it up, too, in court, if it came to it. The only plausible explanation was the newspaper that was once known as The Thunderer had pathetically caved in to pressure from Johnson's Downing Street. The story got traction around the world because there was the collaboration between our political and journalistic classes laid bare for all to see.

The Post journalist heard me out as I talked her through what happened and then she said she didn't understand why The Times had dropped it because it was a great story. I wearily reiterated that a great story about corruption in government on this side of the Atlantic had now become almost by definition one that wasn't going to make it into any of our biggest-selling papers. She said she still didn't understand and I tried to explain how Johnson, the journalist-turned-politician, had so disastrously corroded the boundaries between the fourth estate and the other estates of the realm that most newspapers didn't seem to give a damn any more what he got up to.

In this brave new world, the characters of individual editors started to be tested as never before. The acting editor the night The Times dropped the Carriegate story was Tony Gallagher, who I'd got to know during his years in charge at the Telegraph. It had been him who'd overseen the Telegraph's parliamentary expenses investigation more than a decade ago and that took some guts. I'd occasionally lunch with him after we headed off to different newspapers and he struck me as a fundamentally decent man. He was on the Echo's sister paper in Southampton when I was working in Bournemouth and I'd ask him why we'd got into journalism in the first place: to do good or to do bad? Editing the massively pro-Brexit Sun at the time, he didn't reply. Still, he'd at least tried to get Carriegate into his paper rather than reject it out of hand as had Ted Verity, the editor of the Daily Mail, when Walters offered him first dibs on it.

Verity had been Paul Dacre's choice to succeed Geordie Greig as the Daily Mail's editor. Greig had been leading the charge against Johnson with a succession of front pages highlighting his corruption, and it had, by all accounts, been too much for the paper's owner Lord Rothermere, or at least those who advised him. Verity, doubtless with Dacre whispering in his ear, then began trying to protect Johnson, running editorials telling the readers to 'move on' after each successive scandal. Even when the Prime Minister was quite clearly a dead man walking – when the whole country twigged that lying was a compulsion to him – the Mail was still slavishly backing him and comically demanded, the day after he'd been brought down: 'What the hell have they done?'

The man within

When I'd worked for Dacre, his was a confident, sure-footed newspaper and it was not done ever to offer copy approval – according people who figure in stories the right to vet them ahead of publication – but that was precisely what he demanded when he learnt he was about to figure in a play I'd written about Gina Miller's court case against Theresa May's government called Bloody Difficult Women. Without even the slightest hint of self-parody, he instructed the paper's legal department to barrage my producers with increasingly intimidating letters. I declined these requests precisely because that was the kind of man Dacre – and a great many other editors before him – had made me. Still, those letters – along with the phone call from The Washington Post – were a wake-up call.

What always struck me about Johnson – and all the weakest people I've known in my life – is that ultimately he does not know who he is. I'm beginning to wonder if Dacre knows any more. The greatest editors of recent times – Ben Bradlee of The Washington Post and Harry Evans of The Sunday Times, among them – knew they had to keep a reasonable distance from politicians, and they died as newspapermen. Any objective obituary of Dacre would have to include his frankly demeaning quest to take over as Johnson's choice as the boss of the broadcasting watchdog Ofcom. Dacre doesn't seem to comprehend how he must be making English – the man who gave him the job and who loathed corruption in politics and campaigned passionately for Britain to join the European Union – turn in his grave.

The heart of the matter

It'd be nice to think there'd be a flight to quality journalism in the years ahead, but Johnson has done to the trade what he's done to politics, and now most people will conclude we are all as bad as each other. Trust, once lost, is seldom easy to restore. I don't really care what happens to Johnson, but I think it's unlikely the Telegraph will be willing to give him the kind of salary it had before. I got to know Sir David Barclay well and he told me Johnson was forever on the phone to him, pleading poverty and complaining about his child maintenance payments. Sir David is now dead and the Telegraph's trenchant criticism of Johnson towards the end of his premiership suggests his twin brother Sir Frederick is a better judge of character. Whatever Johnson chooses to do with the rest of his life, he'll mess it up and leave only destruction and despair in his wake.

About the contributor

Tim Walker is a British Press Award-winning journalist, author, and playwright who has worked in senior staff positions for The Observer, Daily Mail and The Daily Telegraph. His debut play Bloody Difficult Women had a sell-out extended run at the Riverside Studios, Hammersmith in spring 2022 before transferring to the Edinburgh Festival. His latest book is Star Turns (SunRise Publishing, September 2021), an anthology of interviews with leading actors that he has conducted over 30 years.

ACT TWO:
THE MAKING
AND BREAKING
OF 'BOJO'

Becoming Boris

John Mair introduces the contributors assessing the media-led rise and fall of Boris Johnson

Those who live by the media die by it. There is no one of whom this is truer than Alexander Boris de Pfeffel Johnson: a journalist turned politician soon to be a journalist again? How much was he made and unmade by the very media who were his strongest cheerleaders?

To begin at the beginning. How did 'Al' to his family become 'Boris' the student, the journalist, and the UK's Prime Minister?

In 'What's in a name? How Alexander de Pfeffel became Boris through the media and with the media' Steven McCabe locates this transition in Johnson's schooldays: that is where he invented 'Boris' to stop himself being bullied. This was also where he invented the clown persona. It worked so it stuck: "Making people laugh was a schtick which served him well at Eton in avoiding the malign intent of bullies. Johnson continued to hone the 'Boris' character whilst at Oxford where he studied Classics and, subsequently, employed it to maximum effect in advancing his 'brand', initially in his journalistic career and, more especially, in politics".

That loveable blond clever rogue 'Boris' persona drove him on to The Daily Telegraph, The Spectator, Parliament, the mayoralty of London, Parliament again, and eventually 10 Downing Street. The Boris Brand was carefully (albeit chaotically) built all along. As an example, the ruffled hair, not initially in the act, is now brought out at each and every event – specially ruffled. 'Brand Boris' has worked right to the bitter end, as

McCabe concludes: "Boris, the 'shapeshifter' par excellence, developed the clown persona to play the fool and become PM. In the process, he played us all as fools".

Tor Clarke is a hack turned academic. Formerly a regional newspaper editor in, amongst other places, Margaret Thatcher's hometown of Grantham in Lincolnshire, he is now a senior academic at the University of Leicester. In 'Was journalist-Prime Minister Boris Johnson brought down by journalism?' he considers whether Boris Johnson was cut down by the work of fellow hacks or simply by pushing his own self-destruct button: 'Once in government Johnson was dealt a terrible hand but proceeded to play it badly. When things went against him or things emerged to his discredit his habit of dissembling and denying just dug all his holes deeper. And in the end his colleagues simply had enough of it'.

Since Partygate reared its jolly head in The Daily Mirror on 30 November 2021, his greatest critics, those who led the pack chasing Johnson down rabbit hole after rabbit hole, was the very pack of political correspondents from whose womb he had been born a journalist thirty years before: 'He failed to remember the public demands integrity from their leaders, of whatever colour. Political journalists are there to question, to explain, to compare, to expose, and to try to find the truth inside the maelstrom of political debate and hard-fought vested interests'.

Clarke concludes, like many others, that it was the lying big which got him in the end: 'Journalism didn't bring Johnson down, it just did its job of holding the powerful to account and his demise was inevitable'.

And now it's time for someone to offer the case for the defence. Robin Aitken is a Daily Telegraph columnist and a big fan of Bojo. In 'The making and unmaking of Boris' he posits that the very platforms on which he came to public prominence – satirical television shows such as Have I Got News For You (HIGNFY) – and on which Johnson was a star turn for several years, boosted the image of Boris the clown but might also have sowed the seeds of his ultimate downfall: 'In Johnson's case the normal rules do not apply; he is, as the lawyers would have it, sui generis, a one-off. What the public saw on HIGNFY was a man who could take a joke at his own expense, a man who could laugh at his own manifest weaknesses, a man apparently lacking in vanity – in short, that most English of character-types 'a good sport.''

In short, he was able to turn public opprobrium to public warmth and recognition: 'Any politician who offers himself up on HIGNFY has a fair idea of what's coming: scorn, ridicule, personal insults, and jocular humiliation – all in the name of entertainment. To go on that show as a politician is the modern equivalent of volunteering to put your head in the stocks whilst encouraging the hoi polloi to throw dung at you; it is quite brave. But this is the forum which allowed Boris to shine; it showed the public a man perfectly at ease with himself and the joke, it turned out, was on his opponents'.

And as to his fall, Aitken blames that on the media and Remainers Revenge: 'Boris' rise and fall holds lessons for all politicians even if very few of them have anything like his unique set of political talents'.

Made in the media, using the media shamelessly, and then being crippled by it. Another act in the Boris tragi-comic opera.

What's in a name?
How Alexander de Pfeffel became Boris

**Boris is not Boris. Simple as that.
It is his stage name for politics, journalism,
and comedy. Steven McCabe explores
the evolution of a brand**

Whilst prominent British politicians attract attention in terms of background and personality, examination of Boris Johnson has been phenomenal. Many believe the persona he portrays in public is an act. Beneath the 'bumbling fool Boris' he's played all his adult life there's a different person. Johnson, it's thought, may be more like the gifted child he was once believed to be. Who is the real person beneath the character he's used as a distraction and mask so successfully? How did the bookish teenager Alexander Boris de Pfeffel Johnson, initially having created the alter ego of 'Boris' as a way to avoid bullying, through clever manipulation and connivance with the media, use it attain the highest political office in the United Kingdom and achieve electoral success for the Conservative Party.

One-name slebs

A signifier of a true celebrity is to be known only by one name. Cher, Bono, Banksy, Eminem, Lulu, Sting and Madonna are well known examples. Though not unknown in politics, being known by one name is less common. After all, in comparison to show business and enter-tainment, politics is usually occupied by those who consider it a serious pursuit. However, one politician, known only his second forename, has intentionally cultivated celebrity and frivolity as part of his popular appeal. Tom McTague, in his Atlantic article 'Boris Johnson Meets His Destiny' published just before he became Prime Minister of the UK on 23 July 2019, a position he'd long coveted and believed to be his right, asserted that the person likely to win the contest to succeed Theresa May was 'far more known than understood'. Whilst explicitly willing to engage in whatever publicity would garner attention, and subject to many stories which he'd be presumed had not appeared, many wondered what really motivated the individual behind the carefully crafted persona.

The birth of a 'fifth Beatle'

Johnson, known to family and close friends as 'Al', revels in his Englishness. However, he was born in America in New York. Political analyst Adam Fleming, in the first of his podcast series, Boris, notes Johnson's birth coincided with Beatlemania. Enjoying a comfortable upper-middle class background, he was subjected to his father's peripatetic career. The family moved 32 times in 14 years within the United States and the UK and then to Brussels in 1973 where he attended the European School. Serving the needs of children of employees of the European Commission, he thrived in the school's liberal learning culture. Johnson was friendly there with Marina, daughter of the BBC's Charles Wheeler. He'd later marry and divorce her.

Alexander the child prodigy invents 'Boris the clown'

At school in Brussels, where pupils were encouraged to think freely, Johnson learned to speak French. According to one biographer Andrew Gimson, he was described by one teacher there as un enfant doué, a gifted child. Sonia Purnell, who worked as deputy head of bureau at The Telegraph when Boris was appointed by Max Hastings as its Brussels correspondent in 1989, and later wrote a highly informative biography of him, says the quiet and studious boy, close to his mother, was deeply affected by being sent to Ashdown House, a traditional English boarding school in England in 1975. As well as having to travel across the Channel without his parents, Johnson was required to wear a uniform and adhere to arcane and ludicrous rules. Purnell believes beatings by staff and fellow pupils were accepted as convention.

Many believe that it was at Ashdown and, more particularly, at Eton, the elite public school which Johnson attended after winning a scholarship by dint of undoubted academic ability, that the germ of recreating himself was born. Finding himself bullied at Eton by fellow students, many of whose wealth and connections to English aristocracy would have made Johnson feel like an interloper, he would no longer be 'Al' but, instead, 'Boris the Clown' who delighted in breaking rules and thumbing his nose as convention (Beard, 2021). According to Purnell, 'Here was the near-perfect prototype of the seemingly bumbling, shambolic persona wrapped round the rapier intellect that we know today'. Making people laugh was a schtick which served him well at Eton in avoiding the malign intent of bullies. Johnson continued to hone the 'Boris' character whilst at Oxford where he studied Classics and, subsequently, employed it to maximum effect in advancing his 'brand', initially in his journalistic career and, more especially, in politics (Kuper, 2022).

Boris the entertainer, a media sensation

In the 1952 British comedy, The Card, Alec Guinness plays the lead role as Edward Henry (Denry) Machin who, though from humble origins, is ferociously ambitious. Through a mixture of willingness to take risks, be unconventional, and make people smile, Denry succeeds in being a 'card', a witty or eccentric individual. Johnson was conscious his family was not fabulously rich or titled, unlike Eton friends such as Charles Spencer, brother of Diana Princess of Wales, and Darius Guppy who'd eventually be convicted of fraud and who played a different game.

Johnson believed himself to be destined for greatness (Cockerell, 2019). In 1987, having enjoyed a bohemian and somewhat libertine three years at Oxford University, Johnson graduated with a 2:1, representing, to him, 'failure'. Johnson acknowledged his persona as 'Boris', a lovable buffoon, had ensured popularity at as a debater, co-editor of satirical magazine Tributary and, on his second attempt, election as Oxford Union President.

Journalism represented an obvious career move for Johnson. His first stint, at The Times as a graduate trainee, ended in calamity with him being sacked in 1988 for making up a quote by his godfather Colin Lucas. His next job, secured through editor Max Hastings, was as a reporter at The Daily Telegraph. This allowed Johnson to employ a highly individualistic style of writing and to be explicitly polemic. There was appeal to Conservative readers. Hastings has subsequently stated in his excoriating criticism, 'I was Boris Johnson's boss: he is utterly unfit to be prime minister', shortly before becoming Prime Minister (2019). This suggests he considered Boris' talents should be practised well away from London.

In 1989, Johnson was sent to Brussels as Telegraph correspondent on the European Commission. By writing stories which were patently nonsense Johnson undoubtedly knew that as well as appealing to the paper's many Eurosceptic readers (Gimson, ibid), he engendered dissent among the Conservatives, then led by Margaret Thatcher. Chris Patten subsequently stated that Johnson was 'one of the greatest exponents of fake journalism' (Fletcher, 2017).

Boris the opinion-former and telly star

Adulation, though countered by the opprobrium he'd eventually be subject to on a scale unprecedented for any UK politician, proved seductive to Johnson. His desire to enhance his reputation by provocative journalism grew markedly. Returning from Brussels to be assistant editor and chief political columnist on the Telegraph, he allowed free rein to opinions which, it seemed, characterised him as a bigot and racist. This was particularly so when he started writing a column for the right-wing magazine The Spectator which he'd go on to edit between 1999 and 2005. A growing reputation as a columnist willing to go beyond accepted standards of journalism achieved his objective of emerging from the relative obscurity of merely being a controversial columnist read by hundreds of thousands to become a media star. This was critical in launching his political career (Sabbagh and Perraudin, 2019).

In a televisual age appearing on national networks, viewed by millions, is vital to those courting popularity. Accordingly, Johnson's appearance in 1998 on the BBC satirical current affairs show, Have I Got News For You, made him a household name. Viewers were charmed by Johnson's schtick of blundering through questions. The buffoon act worked and led to invitations to appear on other programmes cementing Boris as a personality synonymous with fun and frivolity. Politics, where real power existed, was the next inevitable step and, as Tim Montgomerie wrote in the Daily Mail, Johnson became 'Heineken Boris', able to reach voters in a way other Conservatives could not.

The tears of a clown

Boris Johnson has cynically used the mask of the clown to create the persona he wants to be (Docx, 2021). Psychologists posit what's known as 'positive reinforcement' by which you exhibit behaviour which is most likely to elicit reward. Boris, the 'shapeshifter' par excellence, developed the clown persona to play the fool and become PM. In the process, he played us all as fools (McCabe, 2021). Eventually, everyone, including close colleagues, grew frustrated by his act. The fact that his management was chaotic and inconsistent added to the belief that he was a liability in office.

The question is whether Al, the gifted child, may, as some speculate, attempt to reinvent Boris? However, there's a question of what the real person beneath the mask of Boris really consists. Precious few know. Significantly, as Johnson's first wife, Allegra Mostyn-Owen claimed,

'Boris is the public person, but did I meet Al, the private person or Alexander a mixture of the private and public or had I lived with Boris, I never knew' (Bower, 2021).

References

Richard Beard (2021) 'Settling Scores, The Private School Prime Minister Takes his Revenge', Byline Times, 27 December, bylinetimes.com/2021/12/27/settling-scores-the-private-school-prime-minister-takes-his-revenge/, accessed 23 July.

Tom Bower (2021) Boris Johnson The Gambler, London: WH Allen.

Michael Cockerell (2019) 'Boris Johnson: The Irresistible Rise', BBC Two, 9 November.

Edward Docx (2021) 'The clown king: how Boris Johnson made it by playing the fool', The Guardian, 18 March 2021, www.theguardian.com/news/2021/mar/18/all-hail-the-clown-king-how-boris-johnson-made-it-by-playing-the-fool', accessed 25 July.

Adam Fleming (2022) 'Boris, The Early Years: The Fifth Beatle', BBC Podcast, 9 July, www.bbc.co.uk/sounds/play/m0019kxh, accessed 23 July.

Martin Fletcher (2017) 'The joke's over – how Boris Johnson is damaging Britain's global stature', New Statesman, 4 November, www.newstatesman.com/long-reads/2017/11/joke-s-over-how-boris-johnson-damaging-britain-s-global-stature, accessed 24 July.

Andrew Gimson (2012), Boris: The Adventures of Boris Johnson, London: Simon and Schuster.

Max Hastings (2019) 'I was Boris Johnson's boss: he is utterly unfit to be prime minister', The Guardian, 24th June, www.theguardian.com/commentisfree/2019/jun/24/boris-johnson-prime-minister-tory-party-britain, accessed 24 July.

Simon Kuper (2022) Chums: How a Tiny Caste of Oxford Tories Took Over the UK, London: Profile Books.

Steve McCabe (2021) 'Al promised you a miracle – Life under 'Greased Piglet' Johnson', in Populism and the Media, edited by J. Mair, T. Clark, N. Fowler, R. Snoddy, and R Tait, Bury St Edmunds: Abramis Academic Publishing.

Tom McTague (2019) 'Boris Johnson Meets His Destiny', The Atlantic, 22 July, www.theatlantic.com/international/archive/2019/07/boris-johnson-profile/594379/, accessed 23 July.

Tim Montgomerie (2012) 'Can 'Heineken Boris' refresh the voters that other Tories cannot reach?', Daily Mail, www.dailymail.co.uk/debate/article-2136814/London-mayoral-elections-Can-Boris-Johnson-refresh-voters-

Tories-reach.html, accessed 25 July.

Sonia Purnell (2011) Just Boris: The Irresistible Rise of a Political Celebrity, London: Aurum Press.

Dan Sabbagh, and Frances Perraudin (2019) 'Laughter and lies: Johnson's journey from journalist to MP', Guardian, 15 July.

About the contributor

Dr Steven McCabe is Associate Professor at Birmingham City University. He writes and comments regularly in the national and international media on politics and the economy. In the past three years he has edited a number of books including Brexit and Northern Ireland, Bordering on Confusion, English Regions After Brexit: Examining Potential Change through Devolved Power, Exploring the Green Economy: Issues, Challenges and Benefits, Green Manufacturing: What this involves and how to achieve success, How To Stop Rising House Prices and Another Way: A call for a new direction in British foreign policy and defence policy?

Was journalist-Prime Minister Boris Johnson brought down by journalism?

Before the ink was dry on his resignation, conspiracy theories about Boris Johnson's downfall were doing the rounds, among them the idea he was brought down by journalism, rather than by the voters. But at the heart of the PM's removal was his tenuous relationship with the truth, argues Tor Clark

W as it Partygate? Was it Chris Pincher? Was it the Northern Ireland Protocol, or even the Downing Street wallpaper? No in the end – as so often before – it wasn't the scandal, but the cover-up which brought down Prime Minister Boris Johnson in July 2022.

There's a huge irony in the journalist-turned-Prime Minister being hunted down over months by the same media of which he had been a prominent member for so long before entering politics.

But it wasn't vindictive. If journalism is about anything it is trying to find the truth and tell it to readers, viewers, and listeners. So journalism didn't bring Johnson down, it just did its job of holding the powerful to account, and his demise was inevitable unless he had changed his modus operandi on becoming PM – and he didn't.

His resistance to resignation over such a long period is interesting and suggests something about his view of his own profession, as he defied journalistic evidence and clung on in No 10 despite all precedents.

Reverence for truth

Boris Johnson has rarely been out of the news throughout his public career and not at all as PM. Was the criticism fair? Why were journalists so critical?

The answer lies in the nature of journalism itself.

Journalism has many purposes and many definitions. But the late, great campaigning Sunday Times editor Sir Harold Evans perhaps summed up the purpose of journalism best when in response to a request from The Independent to define journalism in a 2004 interview, he replied: 'The object in journalism is reverence for truth'.

And there you had the problem for Prime Minister Johnson. He never seemed to revere the truth very much. As such it set his conduct and reputation on a collision course with journalism.

He made his name as a journalist, ironically enough, by covering the European Union for the Daily Telegraph. But he had lost a previous job for making up quotes in a story.

He was sacked from Michael Howard's Conservative Shadow Cabinet for denying an extra-marital affair.

He has denied an affair with London-based American businesswoman Jennifer Arcuri while he was Mayor of London. She has offered quite a bit of detail on her version of events.

He told EU Referendum voters Brexit would bring huge immediate benefits to the UK and an extra £350m a week to the NHS.

He made light of the intractable problem raised by Northern Ireland being part of Brexit UK while continuing its links to the neighbouring Republic of Ireland within the EU as part of the Good Friday Agreement to protect peace in the six counties.

He was not at all clear who had paid for his new Downing Street wallpaper.

He told the House of Commons there hadn't been any parties.

And the straw that broke the camel's back: he sent out his own ministers to deny he knew about previous misconduct by his Deputy Chief Whip Chris Pincher.

Beyond all that, most bizarrely, he has always refused to tell us how many children he has.

Politicians' attempts to avoid the truth for their own purposes are not new. Jim Callaghan's 'Crisis, what crisis?', Margaret Thatcher's error over the navigational direction of the General Belgrano and, perhaps most notoriously Tony Blair's insistence on the presence of weapons of mass destruction in Iraq, all turned out to be huge issues which have lingered long after the premiership ended, and to an extent have tarnished those prime ministerial reputations.

So politicians are famously accused of being 'economical with the truth' but Johnson's economy was on an industrial scale in comparison with his predecessors.

If journalism is about finding the truth and exposing hypocrisy, politician Boris Johnson's relations with his former profession were always going to be challenging.

Johnson deserves his biggest success

As a Prime Minister and party leader, Johnson deserves the credit for his party's 2019 general election victory. Yes, it was a party victory, but he was the face and embodiment of that party and that campaign at that time. It was his stand-out success and to deny that is churlish.

The photographs of him and his then-fiancé Carrie celebrating victories on the night inside No 10 tell a story of a huge success for his simple message and charismatic campaigning style.

If all political careers end in failure – and his also ended in indignity – then those of us who watch politics must give credit to politicians for their obvious successes.

Johnson led his party to a huge working majority in 2019 when no Tory government in the previous three attempts had won enough MPs to easily get its programme through Parliament.

His victory was soured for the media, his critics, and opponents by his obfuscation over key policy questions at times, plus confiscating a regional reporter's phone, and hiding in an industrial fridge to avoid talking to journalists.

Perhaps the biggest media issue with his ultimately victorious campaign leadership, was his failure to face journalistic inquisitor-in-chief Andrew Neil's primetime BBC election interview programme, when the veteran Rottweiler interviewer had already taken apart his rivals, most notably Johnson's chief opponent, Labour leader Jeremy Corbyn.

The decision not to allow him to face that interview – presuming his party had agreed it with the BBC – when all his rivals took part was disingenuous, but as a calculation to help him win, his communications team probably thought it worth the hit.

As a politician always keen to ad lib for amusement he was kept on a tight rein during the campaign by his message police, and simply kept aiming his 'Get Brexit Done' message relentlessly at the 52 per cent of voters he knew had supported it just three years earlier and against an unconvincing and divided set of opposition parties.

Record in government

Returning to power with his greatly increased popular mandate, he finally got the UK out of the EU, though he hasn't shown anything of the bright future outside the EU he promised and campaigned for, and he was soon wanting to rewrite his own agreement with the EU which achieved the exit.

Mounting evidence – and no doubt testimony to the Covid public inquiry – suggests his government badly handled several parts of the pandemic decision-making, meaning many more people died than should have.

The Covid vaccine roll-out was a huge success, but whose success was it? Johnson's government claimed it but many scientists and public servants were involved in that positive outcome and the politicians don't deserve as much credit as they claim for themselves.

On many occasions – Partygate being the most obvious, but there are many other examples – Johnson would shoot from the hip with a straight denial, an easy answer or an attempt to downplay a serious issue.

The constant fuelling of the Partygate story was interesting and a little sinister as far as his supporters were concerned. Just as one aspect might die down, another piece of video or series of WhatsApp messages would appear to add a new chapter to the unfolding scandal.

But what were journalists supposed to do? Yes, the fire of controversy was being fuelled by Johnson's enemies with vested interests, but the journalists couldn't have been expected to ignore those serious and legitimate new angles to an ongoing story with public interest.

Perhaps if Johnson and all the affected colleagues had just put their hands up and hung their heads at the start and said, 'Yes, we met up and we had drinks when it wasn't allowed and we are sorry', that might have drawn a line under it.

But their failure to do that or acknowledge just how arrogant and offensive their actions seemed to the vast majority of their fellow citizens, many making terrible sacrifices just to stick to the rules, led to a perception they didn't care about their own rules, dragged out the story, and its cumulative effect eventually finished off Boris Johnson.

When the government machine got involved after the Chris Pincher Carlton Club incident and ministers were sent out to defend the indefensible with little evidence, the rot set in among his closest government colleagues. No politician wants to be seen to be knowingly peddling untruths. At the end of Johnson's reign ministers sent out to defend him were prominent among the resignations.

Once in government Johnson was dealt a terrible hand but proceeded to play it badly. When things went against him or things emerged to his discredit his habit of dissembling and denying just dug all his holes deeper. And in the end his colleagues simply had enough of it.

Johnson and journalism: A verdict

In the end, here was a genuinely publicly-recognisable politician, who had achieved the highest office in the land, led a successful insurgent campaign to win the EU Referendum against all the odds and the establishment, then taken on a seemingly impossible situation with Parliament and the EU both deadlocked on Brexit, and proceeded to defy both and win a landslide election victory.

All was set for a parliament – or even two – of unrestrained populist Conservative rule. Yet just two and half years after that incredible electoral success, PM Johnson was humiliated and driven out of office by the people he had appointed to government, despite his belief in the personal nature of his huge electoral mandate.

Many MPs, and certainly a lot of voters and Tory grassroots members, believed that 2019 victory was down to his personality and campaigning style. But despite this, by September 2022 he was just a Conservative backbencher again, albeit one with a lucrative writing and public speaking career ahead of him.

What is the verdict? How can journalism have brought this powerful politician down in the end?

The answer is simply that he failed to remember the public demands integrity from their leaders, of whatever colour. Political journalists are there to question, to explain, to compare, to expose, and to try to find the truth inside the maelstrom of political debate and hard-fought vested interests.

Truth is a vital part of public trust and as long as journalists remember their duty to the truth and the public value it, there is hope its importance in public life can be sustained. In the end it was the truth which did for Prime Minister Johnson. The only mystery is why it took so long.

About the contributor

Tor Clark is Associate Professor in Journalism and Deputy Head of the School of Media, Communication and Sociology at the University of Leicester. He is co-editor of Populism, the Pandemic and the Media: Journalism in the Age of Covid, Trump, Brexit and Johnson, published by Abramis and Routledge in 2021. As a political journalist he has covered eight general elections.

The making and unmaking of Boris

Boris Johnson's success was built on his mastery of the media; but the media is an unreliable friend and no politician's permanent ally and in the end it destroyed his premiership. Robin Aitken explores Johnson's downfall

The Boris Johnson story can be read as a modern morality play. Like Icarus, Boris soared but flew too close to the burning sun and after briefly lighting up the political firmament plunged to earth in a fall as dizzying as his initial climb. And in this iteration of the ancient myth the burning sun that caused his downfall was the media which throughout his career Boris had used and dominated. But, too quickly for his supporters and admirers, the intense glare turned from limelight to death ray and undid him. His rise and fall holds lessons for all politicians even if very few of them have anything like his unique set of political talents.

Has he got news for you?

To understand Boris's ascent to the summit a good place to start is the long-running satirical news show Have I Got News For You. The programme has been a staple of the BBC's offering since 1990, the kind of staying power that only a really successful format bestows. Guided by a host (originally the satirist Angus Deayton) and with its two team captains – Ian Hislop and Paul Merton – holding the show together, HIGNFY invites the audience to indulge in some sharp (often really quite cruel) jokes at the expense of our rulers. Being able, and encouraged, to laugh at those who wield power, is one of those apparently trivial, but in truth vital, hallmarks of a proper democracy; it is delicious for us, the ruled, to see the powerful mocked - and healthy too. No dictatorship would ever tolerate a HIGNFY and it was this show which turbo-powered Johnson's political career.

Between 2002 and 2006 Johnson, then the MP for Henley, was the guest presenter on HIGNFY four times and rewatching those appearances provides valuable insights into the man's unique attributes. Any politician who offers himself up on HIGNFY has a fair idea of what's coming: scorn, ridicule, personal insults, and jocular humiliation – all in the name of entertainment. To go on that show as a politician is the modern equivalent of volunteering to put your head in the stocks whilst encouraging the hoi polloi to throw dung at you; it is quite brave. But this is the forum which allowed Boris to shine; it showed the public a man perfectly at ease with himself and the joke, it turned out, was on his opponents.

Public mockery is an unusual route to the top, public ridicule rarely viewed as a springboard to political success. But in Johnson's case the normal rules do not apply; he is, as the lawyers would have it, sui generis, a one-off. What the public saw on HIGNFY was a man who could take a joke at his own expense, a man who could laugh at his own manifest weaknesses, a man apparently lacking in vanity – in short, that most English of character-types 'a good sport'.

It takes an unusually robust personality and an unusually thick skin to endure being roughed-up on television and go on to prosper – but self-confident resilience was Johnson's secret weapon.

To his detractors (and Johnson has never been short of those) this TV persona of his was part and parcel of a profound fakery; this man was not 'serious', he was too much of a showman – a 'character' without substance; he was loathed, really seriously disliked, not just on the Left but by many in his own party.

Liking Boris and his humour

What really irritated his critics was a popularity they could not understand and which none of them could emulate; because one of the great differences about Johnson is that he was, genuinely, liked. And it was public affection, as much as any policy offering, which twice got him elected as Mayor of London, a city where Labour has ruled the roost for decades. Those victories marked him out as a politician of a different stripe; I can think of no other politician of the past 50 years who connected with the public as he did. He was, in the old litmus test for politicians, the kind of bloke you'd happily share a pint with.

The essential ingredient in his success was that, unlike nearly all his contemporaries, Johnson has a genuine sense of humour. Perhaps other politicians do too but they mostly stay locked away from public view.

Boris's quip about Burka-clad ladies 'looking like letterboxes' had his critics pursing their lips in sententious disdain – lemon-suckers all. But that, oh so incorrect remark, was funny because they actually do resemble letterboxes, so it hit home. His humour and lack of pomposity were among the things that convinced the voters that Johnson was authentic.

That authenticity gained him thumping election victory in December 2019, the best Tory performance since the 1980s, a victory that rested on the conversion of former Labour voters to Boris's cause.

It was Brexit what done it

His victory was underpinned by Brexit. After the disastrous May premiership (in my lifetime May, Anthony Eden, and Gordon Brown are in a photo-finish for the 'worst dud' title) Boris was the only viable candidate, the one person who could complete the Brexit process. In doing so he kept faith with the voters (any outcome other than a proper break with the EU would have destroyed all faith in politics) and wrote his name in the history books. Brexit was his great achievement but simultaneously the root cause of his undoing. Brexit opened the wound which had been plastered over since the accession referendum in 1975 and those on the losing end, the Remainer establishment, held Boris personally responsible. Those for whom membership of the EU was, still is actually, an article of faith – despite the 'democratic deficit' that membership involved – never forgave him. It was they, aided and abetted by their numerous media allies, who eventually did for him.

In the House of Commons, and even more so in the House of Lords, there were permanent majorities who favoured remaining in the EU. A good chunk of the Tory backbenches were always resentful that Johnson had, as they saw it, bamboozled the country into leaving. The charge, endlessly repeated, was that the Leave campaign, with its battle bus emblazoned with the slogan that the cost of membership was £350 million a week, was dishonest; it was too rarely pointed out that the whole Remain case was based on a much bigger lie: that membership of the EU was compatible with national sovereignty and that there was no long-term ambition for the EU to become one super-state.

Battered by the mainstream media

The hostility of the political establishment to Johnson was echoed and amplified by the sustained barrage of abuse he received in the media. In the broadcast media he had few allies: the BBC, Channel 4, and Sky were aligned with the Remain campaign throughout the referendum period itself and their hostility increased when he entered No 10. The BBC's then-political editor Laura Kuenssberg and many of her colleagues showed an almost naked contempt for Johnson but perhaps the most vehement and damaging criticisms came from supposedly Tory-supporting commentators: the likes of Matthew Parris in The Spectator, Max Hastings in The Sunday Times, and Hugo Rifkind in The Times wrote, week after week, about their hatred and contempt for Johnson. Only the Daily Mail stayed supportive until the end.

The Boris party's over

Partygate was his nemesis. The brouhaha conjured up around the socialising that occurred in Downing Street whilst lock-down laws were in place always seemed disproportionate (it was rarely pled in mitigation that the civil servants and politicians involved were among the very few in Whitehall who worked through the pandemic and that the parties were a pretty harmless way of relaxing after weeks under great pressure); but when the media is in full cry, with the quarry visible and running, there could only be one outcome.

The media, which Johnson had so skilfully used in the years of his advancement, turned on him with ferocity and eventually ran their fox to ground.

Johnson was, it turned out, fundamentally ill-suited to the job of Prime Minister; his skill-set, which served him so well as a campaigner, was of less value when he achieved power; and his 'good sport' persona never worked its charm on his Parliamentary colleagues. But it seemed, to this observer anyway, that he lacked the necessary managerial skills to construct an effective administration; a more cautious and controlling individual would never have countenanced those parties, innocuous though they were. But then a more cautious and controlling person would never have seen Brexit through in the way Johnson did; his very strengths – his fun-loving spirit, his generally unbuttoned approach to life, his risk-taking – turned out to be the weaknesses that brought him down.

Johnson's short tenure at No 10 ended in chaos and confusion with ministers resigning in droves, the media in uproar and the pungent aroma of schadenfreude emanating from his critics.

But Boris Johnson will have left a deeper mark on the nation than many Prime Ministers who enjoyed much longer periods in office. His 'crimes' were really petty misdemeanours but they gave his enemies enough ammunition to bring him down; his downfall was the revenge of the Remainers who surfed the wave of synthetic outrage the media created. But Brexit feels permanent now; it will be a brave and foolhardy party that reopens that divisive question again and Boris Johnson will be guaranteed a place in the history books as the man who set the United Kingdom free from a supra-national entity to which it had been deceitfully shackled.

About the contributor

Robin Aitken is a Daily Telegraph columnist. He was a BBC correspondent reporting on programmes such as The World Tonight.

ACT THREE: THE RIGHT-WING PRESS LINE UP BEHIND JOHNSON

Stand by your man

This Act examines Boris Johnson's relationship with the UK's right-wing press. It's often assumed that the Express titles, the Mail titles, the Star, the Telegraph titles, and the Times slavishly supported him but a close examination of them reveals something far less consistent, indeed at times almost even schizophrenic. As a curtain-raiser to this Act, Paul Connew offers a close reading of these titles as they veered from celebration of Johnson to denunciation and back

S tand By Your Man, the old Tammy Wynette country classic, must have haunted the minds of right-wing newspaper editors at regular intervals in 2022 when it came to the thorny subject of Boris Johnson. Should it be a statement of intent or an open question? Blind love and loyalty versus objective criticism? Flawed hero still or disgraced zero? Either way, schizophrenia came to the fore as the mood music became ever more discordant. At times it even affected Bojo's most loyal newspaper champion, Paul Dacre's Daily Mail and Mail on Sunday.

The headlines reflected the schizophrenia level as Wallpapergate morphed into Sleazegate, then Partygate, then Gropegate, till the gates of political hell opened for the man they virtually deified over Brexit and that 2019 election landslide.

Take the Mail titles, for example. The early days of Partygate featured Boris-damning headlines like 'ONE RULE FOR THEM, NEW RULES

FOR THE REST OF US' (9 December 2021) and 'Can even Boris the greased piglet wriggle out of this?' (6 July 2022) while at the same time rediscovering its love affair with the Prime Minister before responding to the damning Sue Gray report with stories such as 'Sorry, there'll be no hangin' today. Release the prisoner!' (Henry Deedes, 25 May 2022). The Daily Express, equally besotted with standing by its man Boris, took a similar Page One stance with 'Really …. Is This What All The Fuss Is About?' (26 May 2022). Not that the Express, whose credibility and influence declines at the same rate as its circulation figures, carries the clout of the Mail. The Mail's determination to try and save Johnson extended to a front page picture of him looking statesmanlike with the splash headline 'Boris Stares Down the Mutiny' (7 July 2022) and insisting he still has 'his mandate from 14m voters'. In another it branded the MPs who rebelled against their man a 'narcissistic rabble'.

But even the Mail titles weren't immune from schizophrenia and inconsistency when it came to matters Johnson. On 3 July it was the Mail on Sunday who broke on its front page the revelation that Boris had known about the proclivities of his crony and deputy chief whip Chris Pincher for two years despite earlier strenuous denials. But the following day's Daily Mail appeared horrified by its sister title's journalistic scoop and loudly told its reader: 'Boris Johnson is still the best man to lead Britain', a position both titles have since stuck to, apparently at the direction of Paul Dacre himself.

The supreme irony here, of course, is that it was Pinchergate/Gropegate (take your pick) that proved the coup de grace for Boris's premiership, the catalyst for almost 60 of his MPs and ministers to demand his departure.

Jane Martinson, professor of journalism at City University, London and long-time Guardian columnist, asked the pertinent question in her 7 July column headlined: 'Why did the Daily Mail support Johnson long after other press allies turned their back?' Wrote Martinson: 'A newspaper that styles itself as a bastion of middle England morality should have been the first to ask hard questions of a doomed leader. Standing up for decency and family values as well as a prime minister who does neither is a bad look for a newspaper that likes to think of itself as the minister for morality.'

Pointedly, Martinson drew attention to the speech Mail owner Lord Rothermere made to 800 guests at the paper's 125th birthday party in May 2022, lauding its 'tradition of exposing incompetent and immoral politicians' and urging all newspapers 'We must not be afraid to call out the charlatans.' Quite a few Mail staffers of my acquaintance choked on that one!

Those of us with long memories can recall how it was the Daily Mail under Paul Dacre's first editorship who repeatedly exposed Boris Johnson's amorality and won a 2013 Appeal Court victory over the right to expose the married mayor's fathering of a child by art expert Helen Macintyre. How curiously times change between immoral Mayor of London to all is forgiven Prime Minister, eh?

Mail insiders insist the support for Johnson also stems from the majority view of its readers via letters and online feedback, although how scientific that is remains somewhat unclear. And the paper's strong advocacy for Liz Truss in the summer 2022 leadership election was based on her 'Continuity Boris' characterisation along with her unsubtle attempts to portray herself as Margaret Thatcher reborn. Ironically, most surviving members of Thatcher Cabinets, along with the majority of economists, shared the Times' view that Rishi Sunak reflected a more Thatcherite platform on the economy.

Certainly the Mail's dogged loyalty to Big Dog hasn't been the dog whistle sounded by other pro-Conservative titles as the scandal count mounted and the opinion polls showed a massive collapse in trust and how seriously that was damaging the Tory brand and its re-election prospects.

In August 2022 the Mail titles' defence of Boris reached an extraordinary apogee. They threw their weight behind the Johnson camp's demand for the Privileges Committee inquiry into whether he misled parliament – which could expel him as an MP – to be abandoned. Picking up on Nadine Dorries and Zac Goldsmith's pleas for the Committee to abandon its inquiry the Mail on Sunday and Daily Mail invoked Trump with headline references to 'witch-hunt' and 'kangaroo court'.

The Times has been on a clear anti-Boris line since early spring 2022 and threw its weight behind Rishi Sunak's bid to replace him, despite the 'back stabber' chorus from the party's right-wing inside and outside parliament. While the Times' Murdoch stablemate The Sun veered unsteadily between cheerleading for Boris and criticising him, even at the height of the Partygate furore, it often buried stories well back in the paper. This was perhaps partly explained by embarrassment over its appointment of former No 10 aide James Slack as deputy editor whose boozy Downing Street leaving party on the eve of Prince Philip's funeral sent public outrage into overdrive. That said, it was the Sun and its young political reporter Noa Hoffman who first broke the 'Pinchergate' scandal that ultimately sealed Boris Johnson's fate.

For its part, Boris's old paymaster the Daily Telegraph swayed between support and condemnation, but with the latter increasingly prominent as the evidence of its former golden boy's incompetence, dishonesty, and abuse of power piled up. Slowly, but surely, sycophancy was being replaced by cynicism, albeit of the self-interest variety. A Press Gazette research study in May across all UK national daily and Sunday titles found 41% were largely negative about Boris Johnson, 33% were neutral, and 26% positive, but tilted by a positivity count of 91% in the Mail titles and 70% in the Daily Express and Sunday Express. The Telegraph only totted up 24% on the positivity front, with the Times lower still at 13%, although 66% were deemed neutral.

Johnson himself, word has it, was particularly shaken and annoyed by the Telegraph giving huge prominence to John Major's scathing attack on him, in which the former prime minister indicted Bojo on charges of eroding public trust in British democracy, showing contempt for ministerial standards, damaging the UK's international reputation, and attacking civil rights and liberties. And that was way back in February 2022.

But somehow it was that most tabloid of tabloids the Daily Star, whose front pages often display a wacky satirical genius, who summed it up best for me. Over a tombstone alongside a frazzled looking Boris it read: 'Here lies the prime minister's credibility. And lies and lies and lies and lies and lies and lies and lies and lies and lies and lies'.

Now read on for the takes of Ray Snoddy, Professor Julian Petley, Liz Gerard, and Professor Brian Cathcart on the Chronicles of Boris and the British Press.

The right-wing British press got their man into Number 10, and then lost him

The right-wing press were largely responsible for making Boris Johnson, and, when nemesis came, were similarly responsible. Raymond Snoddy analyses the rise and fall of Boris Johnson in the pages of those newspapers

By any standards Thursday 7 July was one of the most dramatic days in recent British political history, at least since the resignation of Margaret Thatcher in 1990. That morning the Daily Mail, loyal to the last, reported that Prime Minister Boris Johnson intended to 'stare down' the mutiny and was still insisting he would not give up 'his mandate from 14 million voters'.

The Mail was so desperate to hold on to Johnson because its top editorial leadership remained convinced that he was the one most capable of beating Labour leader Sir Keir Starmer in the next general election, despite Johnson's accumulating baggage.

Later that morning he resigned as leader of the Conservative Party, though not yet as Prime Minister, swept away by an unstoppable tide of Cabinet and ministerial resignations.

Our man lost it

The next morning it was the Daily Mail which best summed up the instincts of the right-wing press which had been so instrumental in Johnson's rise to power and his ability to hold on to Downing Street for nearly three years despite a succession of scandals that would have brought down any of his predecessors.

'What the Hell Have They Done?' was the Mail's splash headline embellished with the implications of it all: 'With a consoling hug from Carrie and Wilf, Boris is cast out by a party in the grip of collective hysteria. Keir Starmer is cock-a-hoop. Corks are popping in Brussels – and Moscow. And the Tories don't have a clue who should replace him'.

The paper attacked the 'utterly duplicitous' Nadhim Zahawi for accepting the post of Chancellor of the Exchequer one moment and telling Johnson to go the next, while the Mail on Sunday had its knives out for former Chancellor Rishi Sunak who led the spate of resignations.

Other Conservative supporting newspapers such as The Sun and The Daily Telegraph allowed themselves to be more critical of Johnson's endless unforced errors but were convinced he had still been a great Prime Minister because of the big calls he had got right, as they saw it – everything from delivering an 80-seat Conservative majority and 'getting Brexit done', to the Covid vaccine response and his enthusiastic support for Ukraine in the face of the Russian invasion.

Our man is still our hero

Johnson may have been 'flawed' but according to The Sun was still 'a giant figure in our nation's story, the most significant politician since Margaret Thatcher'.

There was no mea maxima culpa, as he put it, either from Alister Heath, editor of the Sunday Telegraph. Johnson had been the right choice in 2019 because he saved Britain from Corbyn and the Remainers. The Prime Minister's subsequent performance may have been 'atrocious, delusional and indefensible' as he used his Brexit triumph to impose 'socialism and eco-extremism' on the UK. Despite such failures, according to Heath, Johnson will be remembered as one of this country's most consequential Prime Ministers.

Despite such instant certainties Boris Johnson's place in history will take some time to crystallise and is far from certain. Inquiries are still going on into whether he misled the House of Commons on multiple occasions and it is not impossible that he might yet be charged with the criminal offence of misdemeanour in public office.

An official inquiry into the Covid-19 pandemic will almost certainly look at whether Johnson delayed action on lockdowns for too long and then lifted restrictions too early with fatal consequences. Then there is the £37 billion spent on what many saw as a failed Covid Test and Trace system, plus lucrative orders placed with donors to the Conservative Party often for defective equipment.

The claim that his finest achievement was 'Getting Brexit Done' could also face increasing scrutiny in the face of everything from a catastrophic 15 per cent drop in UK trade, and instability in Northern Ireland because of the border on the Irish sea Johnson vowed would never happen, to embarrassing queues at Britain's ferry ports as French officials inevitably check and stamp passports of those coming from a non-EU country.

We made our man

The greatest irony of all is that the phenomenon that is Boris Johnson was largely created by the right-wing nationals, and that they were also responsible for nemesis when it arrived at last.

The Daily Telegraph is probably more guilty than any for ultimately smoothing Johnson's path to 10 Downing Street. For years the paper happily published ridiculous, or grossly exaggerated stories out of Brussels, from bent bananas, and the size of condoms in Italy, to a tale that the European Commission was going to build the world's tallest building for its new headquarters and blow up the old one. Three decades later the refurbished Berlaymont headquarters remain.

The Johnsonian Euro-sceptic stories were often followed up by the rest of the British popular press helping to create a culture of Euro-scepticism in the British public mind that, with the help of Nigel Farage and Ukip, helped to pave the way towards a Brexit referendum victory in 2016 and an election victory for Johnson in 2019. Sir Max Hastings, his editor at the time, was scathing about Johnson before the 2019 election and warned he was totally unsuited to be Prime Minister of this country. Sir Max predicted that a Johnson's Premiership 'would almost certainly reveal a contempt for the rules, precedent, order and stability'. After Johnson's downfall Sir Max added: 'We have had government by clown and it is not funny.'

In recent years the Daily Telegraph gave him a lucrative £265,000 a year perch as a columnist when he was out of office and supported not just his Premiership but hailed his great achievement at 'getting Brexit done'.

The party's over for our man. Whip out

The writing was already on the wall over Partygate thanks to the reporting of the scandalous multiple breaches of lockdown restrictions in Downing Street, with pictures to prove it by Pippa Crear of the Daily Mirror and Paul Brand of ITV.

Yet it looked as if Johnson was managing to shrug off the matter with just a single fixed penalty fine from the Metropolitan Police although polls showed that he had suffered huge reputational damage in the minds of the populace as a result.

It was Johnson's handling of the curious case of the deputy chief Whip Chris Pincher that proved a scandal too far. It was The Sun that broke the story of the pinching Pincher while the Mail on Sunday reported that Johnson had described the Whip as 'handsy, that's a problem. Pincher by name Pincher by nature', before promoting him to the Whips office. It was that promotion, and Johnson's denial of any specific knowledge about Pincher's behaviour beforehand, that ultimately caused his Premiership to unravel.

The political history of these strange times will record that the coup de grace on that momentous Tuesday morning came in the form of a letter to the Parliamentary Commissioner for Standards by Lord McDonald, the former permanent secretary at the Foreign Office who then put the story out on Twitter at 7.30am. The crossbench peer said it was untrue that no formal complaints had been made against Pincher. Complaints had been investigated and upheld. Crucially Johnson had been briefed in person about the affair, blowing apart the Downing Street line that the Prime Minister had not been aware about 'specific allegations'.

Lord McDonald then appeared on BBC Radio Four's Today programme at 8.10am – the time when most of the UK's political class are listening. He explained calmly to Today presenter Nick Robinson exactly how he knew Johnson had been briefed in person by a senior Cabinet official: 'because that official told me so at the time'.

Lord McDonald went on to explain why he had decided to go public on such a sensitive issue. "It is very unusual for a retired official to do what I have done this morning. I've done it by myself because what I've seen and read over the past few days, I knew to be wrong. It gets to the point where you have to do the right thing," he said.

It was an electrifying moment in radio news and political history made all the more powerful because it was understated, unemotional and, for Johnson, dangerously precise.

Our man's friends desert him

The trickle of resignations turned into a flood that swept Johnson's Premiership away within a few hours.

After the period of political mourning was over the big problem for the owners of the right-wing newspapers and their websites was who to back in the rather strange dual election system by which the Conservative party chooses its new leaders.

Now in the second stage where the 160,000 or so Party members get to decide on the two candidates chosen by Conservative MPs where newspapers might have some influence on the outcome.

There is little detailed up-to-date information on what newspapers Conservative members read but it is likely that the paper of choice by a big margin is the Daily Telegraph, followed by the Daily Mail ,The Times, and the Daily Express. In this middle-class demographic The Sun counts for very little.

Early on, the low tax Daily Mail started to let its preferences show in extensive coverage of Foreign Secretary Liz Truss's claim to be 'the unity candidate' with the True Blue agenda, amid warnings that those involved should 'forget Rishi's jam tomorrow' and listen instead to the Truss plea to help voters now.

The Times took a more analytical approach, warning on 23 July that while Truss may have captured the headlines with her promises of tax cuts the public had a right to know why she has changed her mind so often on many important issues. Columnist James Forsyth argued that if the Tories wanted a genuine Thatcherite candidate it has to be Sunak.

Who will Murdoch anoint as our next man/woman?

Which way will Rupert Murdoch jump, or to be more precise where will he decide his best interests lie? The Sun will probably support the populist Truss although The Times may line up behind Sunak who would be the preference of many of its more fiscally conservative readers (deliberate small c).

Unfortunately at the beginning of August, as the ballot papers started arriving, the choice became more problematic for the newspaper proprietors when The Times reported that a private poll for the Truss camp found that the gap between the two candidates was narrowing with the Foreign Secretary now only five points ahead of Sunak with 9 per cent of Conservative members still undecided, though later polls suggested Truss was building on her lead. They may have to wait a little longer before identifying a winning bandwagon to jump on.

A summer devoted to the Conservative leadership campaign will, at least, give a breathing space to Sir Keir, cleared of any wrongdoing involving a beer and takeaway curry in Durham, and who has maintained a double-digit poll lead in recent months.

Once the right-wing press have got their new leader they will turn their guns on the Labour leader and – for them –two new inviting targets. As the blue-on-blue battle raged Sir Keir committed a Labour Government to end non-dom status, which will infuriate the non-dom right-wing newspaper proprietors, and to end charitable status for public schools.

When Boris Johnson's Premiership finally ends on 6 September British media politics could be about to get more vicious whoever emerges victorious from the Conservative leadership election.

About the contributor

Raymond Snoddy, OBE, is the former Media Editor of The Times and the Financial Times. His publications include: The Good, the Bad and the Unacceptable: the Hard News about the British Press (Faber & Faber 1993), Greenfinger: the rise of Michael Green and Carlton Communications (Faber & Faber 1996), and It Could Be You: the Untold Story of the National Lottery (Faber & Faber 2001). He is now a freelance writer.

The hollow man and the
treacherous watchdog

**Julian Petley argues that the defining features of
Boris Johnson's journalism, namely shameless
self-promotion and a contempt for the truth,
have also characterised his political career.
He also puts forward the view that, far from holding
Johnson to account as PM, as the national press
in a democratic society should be expected to do,
significant sections of that press paved Johnson's
path to power and tried to keep him there in spite
of overwhelming evidence that he
was utterly unworthy of that post**

Even Boris Johnson's severest critics cannot bring themselves to condemn utterly his particular brand of journalism. Thus, for example, in his excoriation of Johnson in The Assault on Truth, Peter Oborne rather surprisingly hails him as 'by some margin the most brilliant political journalist of his generation, with a talent that at times crossed over the line to genius'. Similarly, his former editor at the Telegraph, Max Hastings, in the course of a number of devastating critiques, has also praised him as 'a magnificent journalist' (Mail, 10 October 2012) and 'a great journalist and entertainer' (Mail, 1 July 2016).

It's also interesting that, according to Sonia Purnell in Just Boris, when Johnson was the Telegraph's Brussels bureau chief in the early 1990s and churning out the 'Euromyths' that would launch his journalistic career, Hastings would regularly send him 'herograms', congratulatory notes that Johnson would then paste up as a triumphal arch over his office doorway.

The rat pack

Oborne has even credited, albeit not in a remotely positive sense, Johnson's Brussels myth-making as the invention of 'a new form of journalism' and 'a new school of reporting', arguing that he 'reinvented political language and discourse'. Given the rat pack quality of much of the British press, these myths soon came to dominate all Tory papers, but, given their anti-EU stance, which became far more pronounced during and after Jacques Delors' presidency of the European Commission, if Johnson had not invented the template, then other journalists would most certainly have done so. Indeed, many people still (wrongly) credit the Sun as their progenitor.

Oborne also claims that 'at the heart of his reporting work was a repudiation of the ethics that until then had defined journalist values at Westminster: fairness, accuracy, scruple, scepticism, fact-checking'. He is certainly correct that Johnson's Brussels journalism abandoned normal journalistic ethics, but in fact these had been long absent from significant sections of Fleet Street (even if practised by certain honourable individual journalists on right-wing papers, notably including Oborne himself).

The myth makers

In point of fact, Johnson's stories were simply the latest iteration of a kind of journalism that has a long and dishonourable history in sections of the UK national press, namely myth-making. For example, in the previous decade these self-same papers had concocted vast numbers of equally lurid myths about 'loony left' London councils banning numerous practices – such as schoolchildren singing 'Baa Baa Black Sheep' – on the grounds that they were allegedly racist. But all of these turned out on investigation to be either wildly distorted or indeed wholly false, as I demonstrate in my chapter on such myths in Culture Wars: The Media and the British Left. Furthermore, long before this assault on the urban left, which can now clearly be seen as prefiguring the current press war on 'woke' and the 'liberal elite', such papers had used this weapon against striking workers, immigrants, 'scroungers', travellers, and all the other targets on their long list of hate groups.

It's the way he tells 'em

As far as Johnson's journalistic style is concerned, he had begun to hone this on the Telegraph even before he went to Brussels. Purnell notes his use of 'gloriously old-fashioned phrases, words and humour' and his seasoning of his copy with 'the odd Wodehousian "crumbs" or "cripes" tailored nicely to go with the bumbling persona he was busy perfecting for public consumption'. As Matthew Flinders points out in his contribution to the Hansard Society volume Britain Votes: the 2019 General Election:

Johnson's speeches and articles resonate not because of what he has to say but because of the way he says it, while critics respond in ways that simply heighten his visibility and populist appeal [...] The genius of Johnson's carefully contrived performative act is that it leads opponents to make the mistake of dismissing him as a buffoon while large sections of the public find him endearing.

And, of course, crucial to his populist appeal was the whole pantomime of the carefully crafted 'Boris' schtick which he confected whilst at Eton and performed with aplomb at Oxford and ever afterwards. However, particularly given the benefits of a classical education in which Johnson would certainly have studied rhetoric, none of the stylistic tricks which he employs in his journalism are that difficult to master, especially as he has an entirely cavalier attitude to the truth and will say anything that sounds good and helps to establish a rapport with his readers. Furthermore, he would have been perfectly well aware that his Brussels stories were highly marketable, and thus career-enhancing and financially rewarding. This is because, for reasons both ideological and economic, they would be catnip to the kind of newspapers whose idea of journalism, and particularly op-ed pieces, is simply to tell their readers what their editors and proprietors think that they want to hear and to confirm them in their prejudices.

'Only the winning'

The available evidence suggests that, in his Brussels days, Johnson's amb-itions, vaulting though they were, did not actually extend much beyond the journalistic sphere. He does not appear to have been an EU hater in the Bruges Group mould, and, if anything, his sympathies seem to have leaned in the opposite direction. But as Sonia Purnell, who worked with Johnson in Brussels (an experience she describes as 'joyless' and a 'trial of endurance'), recalled in the Guardian, 15 July 2019:

> There were already clues that it was only the winning, the exercising of supremacy over others, that really mattered. A lack of real conviction about Europe or most other matters seemed to translate into a lack of ideas beyond his own self-projection – what was the point of winning but the winning itself. Johnson never seemed really to believe what he was writing or saying. His motivation seemed solely to boost his own fame and fortune, having identified a lucrative 'gap in the market'.

However, as anti-EU sentiment intensified in the Tory party, Johnson's reporting of EU matters, now from London rather than Brussels, and for the Spectator as well as the Telegraph, came to focus less on trivia such as alleged threats to the 'British banger' and more on the apparent peril to national sovereignty posed by EU membership. And by 2011, the year of the Euro crisis brought on by the indebtedness of countries such as Greece, Spain, and Italy, by which time he was Mayor of London, Johnson was, as Purnell puts it, 'swiftly launching himself as [the Eurosceptics'] obvious chief, the natural-born king of the Conservative Party's Right-wing, once again in the ascendant'.

But the question of whether his journalism on this subject reflected a principled position or was simply the result of political opportunism and overweening ambition remains an open one – particularly in light of the two pieces that he wrote for the Telegraph during the Refer-endum campaign in 2016, one urging readers to vote Remain, the other Leave. In the end the latter was published, but such is Johnson's hollowness that it is quite possible that each represented his views equally accurately, that is, at the moment of writing.

The Tory press/Tory government nexus

But then this glaring example of all that is worst in British journalism eventually went on to become Prime Minister in 2019, coming to exemplify all that is worst in British, and especially English, politics. Johnson's approaches to journalism and politics are identical, and equally contemptuous and destructive of decent standards in each2. As Nick Cohen pointed out in the Observer, 9 July 2022, his modus operandi in both fields was to:

> Showboat with a dramatic pose that strokes the prejudices of your readers. Don't worry if your big idea is impractical or your propositions are false. Ignore facts that spoil the argument and lie without shame if you must. When the complaints come in, shift the blame by branding your critics as bores at best and the mouthpieces of special interests at worst.

Even whilst serving as MP for Henley, followed by London Mayor and then MP for Uxbridge and South Ruislip, Johnson carried on writing for Tory newspapers and the Spectator, thus completely obliterating the conventional line between journalism and politics in a manner which would be unthinkable in most western press cultures. And once he became Prime Minister the symbiotic relationship between the

Tory press and the right-wing of the Tory party became so inextricably intertwined as to constitute an entirely self-contained, self-reinforcing nexus. The term 'client press' doesn't even begin to describe the support that Johnson has received from the Telegraph, Sun, Mail, and Express, and the reciprocal favours that he has bestowed on them, both en route to Number Ten and during his occupancy of it. As Cohen claims:

> With occasional honourable exceptions, they were an active and willing arm of the Johnsonian state. They gave the prime minister a privatised propaganda service complete with cheerleaders, excuse-makers, bullies and spies. Johnson was one of their own. They loved him for it.

And it is already abundantly clear that they were key players in propagating the 'betrayal' and 'stab in the back' narrative which Johnson so assiduously concocted after his resignation from the post of Prime Minister.

When a politician who cares little or nothing for the truth becomes Prime Minister there is a particularly urgent need for a press that is prepared at every turn to expose his lies and evasions, as well as those of his government. Tragically for our democracy, however, significant sections of our press have played an absolutely crucial role in paving this charlatan's path to power and then doing their utmost to try keep him there in the face of all the evidence that he is utterly unfit for the job. This isn't the watchdog that didn't bark – this is the watchdog that let the burglar in, helped him ransack the house, and held the owner at bay whilst he did so.

Endnotes

A vast list of these, complete with explanations in each case of why they are myths, can be found at wayback.archive-it.org/11980/ 20191016145717/blogs.ec.europa.eu/ECintheUK/euromyths a-z-index/ Last accessed 30 July 2022.
See Peter Oborne's annotated list, 'The lies, falsehoods and misrepresentations of Boris Johnson and his government' at boris-johnson-lies.com/ Last accessed 30 July 2022.

References

Nick Cohen (2022) 'With him right until the very end, the Tory press who loved Johnson as one of their own', Observer, 9 July. Available online at www.theguardian.com/commentisfree/2022/jul/09/with-him-to-very-end-tory-press-loved-boris-johnson-one-of-their-own. Last accessed on 30 July 2022.

James Curran, Ivor Gaber, Julian Petley (2019) Culture Wars: The Media and the British Left, 2nd edition, London: Routledge.

Matthew Flinders (2020) 'Not a Brexit election? Pessimism, promises and populism "UK style"', in Jonathan Tonge, Stuart Wilks-Heeg, and Louise Thompson (eds), Britain Votes: the 2019 General Election, Oxford: Oxford University Press/Hansard Society, pp. 225-42.

Peter Oborne (2021) The Assault on Truth: Boris Johnson, Donald Trump and the Emergence of a New Moral Barbarism, London: Simon & Schuster.

Sonia Purnell (2012) Just Boris: A Tale of Blond Ambition, London: Aurum Press.

Sonia Purnell (2019) 'Boris Johnson is about to inherit a crisis his EU-bashing helped spawn', Guardian, 15 July. Available online at www.theguardian.com/commentisfree/2019/jul/15/boris-johnson-inherit-crisis-eu-bashing. Last accessed 30 July 2022.

About the contributor

Julian Petley is honorary and emeritus professor of journalism at Brunel University London. He is a member of the editorial board of the British Journalism Review, and regularly contributes to sites such as Inforrm, Hacked Off, and openDemocracy. He is a co-author of Culture Wars: The Media and the British Left (Routledge 2019), and his most recent publication is a contribution to the edited collection Judicial Independence under Threat (British Academy/Oxford University Press 2022). He is currently co-editing the Routledge Companion to Censorship and Freedom of Expression.

Bojo falls:
What the papers
(even the Tory ones) say

The UK has a right-wing national press, slavishly so at times. During the fall of 'World King' Johnson, they were conflicted: should he stay or should he go? Liz Gerard monitors the opinion-formers in crisis

The party's over, declared the Mirror in January when the Downing Street lockdown gatherings were exposed, and again after Boris Johnson survived a vote of confidence among his MPs.

'It's over' wrote The New European's Tim Walker when the Mail on Sunday splash reported that the Prime Minister had been warned two years ago about Chris Pincher's behaviour.

The wallpaper, the Caribbean holiday, the care homes, the parties, the sex scandals, the fraud scandals, the cronyism, the treehouse, the private jet, the constant dissembling: there have been so many 'crimes' and so many occasions over the past three years when Johnson's media critics rubbed their hands and said 'He can't survive this'. And they had been wrong.

The Mirror and Guardian must have thought it was slam dunk when the Partygate scandal broke and grew – there is still an ongoing investigation into whether the Prime Minister deliberately misled Parliament – but he weathered that storm.

Walker concluded in his Mandrake column for The New European that the MoS lead showed that the most powerful media brand in the country had turned against its man and that his number must therefore be up. Rothermere had, he reported, berated his editors for being out of touch with the country's opinion on Johnson, and this had signalled a dramatic U-turn. The next day the daily ran a leader declaring Johnson 'still the best man to lead Britain'.

But now he's gone (for now at least). Forced out because a lie about someone else's sexual transgression was too much for his Buckeroo party – already overburdened with mistruths, obfuscations, falsehoods, whoppers and fibs – to bear.

In other times, the resignations of two senior Cabinet ministers would have meant the writing on the wall could no longer be painted over. But this was Johnson, so even when Sajid Javid and Rishi Sunak quit, the headlines were equivocal. Rightly so, as it turned out – he went neither quietly nor quickly, leaving dead-tree journalists struggling to keep up and remain relevant. It wasn't only Johnson who could be described by Susie Dent's word of the day, 'filipendulous' or 'hanging by a thread', as the Telegraph splash had it. The Times, Guardian, FT and Independent all said he was 'on the brink', while the Mirror and i were bolder with the 'endgame'.

Is Boris dead or just resting?

The loyalists weren't giving up though. The Sun had Johnson in the 'last chance saloon', a feeble and clichéd headline for which it was chastised on Twitter by former editor Kelvin MacKenzie, while the Express continued its on-another-planet approach (and its weird philosophy on punctuation) with 'Boris fights on! Declaring … I'm now free to cut taxes'. The Mail was less confident, asking 'Can even Boris the Greased Piglet wriggle out of this?' The Greased Piglet? That's the Prime Minister we're talking about here.

The next night, with more than 60 ministerial resignations in 36 hours, and the sacking of Michael Gove, for most it looked as though he really had run out of line, but Johnson was digging in and there was an even greater reluctance to call it on the front pages.

The Mirror and Metro were losing patience and both went for the neat 'Get exit done' line, the Times had Johnson fighting for his life, and the Telegraph had him mortally wounded. But the loyalists still weren't giving up hope. The Mail said he was 'staring down' the mutiny, the Express accepted his 'me or political oblivion' argument (swiftly forgotten after he quit in favour of its usual 'everything's brilliant for the Tories' narrative), and the Sun had the defiant 'You'll have to dip your hands in blood to get rid of me'.

Of course they were all on a hiding to nothing. Whatever they printed was bound to be overtaken by events and by 9am, word was out that the Downing Street lectern would be in position by lunchtime.

What was striking that morning was the bullish attitude of the white tops even at the death. The Express not only had spreads headlined 'PM has mandate for 14m people to get the job done' and 'Boris clings to power with remarkable tenacity', but also a leader applauding his willingness to fight to the bitter end and a Leo McKinstry op-ed suggesting that if Johnson could recapture his buccaneering spirit he might yet survive. The Mail meanwhile had a full-page leader proclaiming that he 'still stood head and shoulders above any of his would-be assassins'. It also devoted two pages to blaming 'Remainiacs' – notably the former senior civil servant Lord McDonald, whose intervention over Chris Pincher precipitated the crumbling Cabinet house of cards – and 'bureaucrats deranged by hatred of Brexit' for the fall of its hero.

Both took up Johnson's line that he had a mandate from 14 million people, which others, including the Telegraph and Times, debunked. As the latter pointed out, we have a parliamentary, not presidential system. Those people voted for a Conservative government, not a particular leader. It's also worth pointing out that 14 million out of an electorate of more than 47 million is hardly a majority; quite the reverse: more voted against the Tories than for them.

The Daily Mail and Boris' morality

The Express has ever been slavishly loyal to every Conservative leader, so its devotion to 'Boris' has never been surprising.

There has always, however, been something deeply uncomfortable and incongruous about the Mail's attitude to his premiership. Everything about his character is alien to all the paper stands for. This is a man who was sacked at least three times for lying, a man who agreed to have a journalist beaten up. Imagine a Labour prime minister moving his lover (the Mail would call her his 'mistress') into No 10, and announcing her pregnancy on the same weekend he had been absent from work negotiating his divorce settlement with his wife of 27 years.

Then look at his behaviour in office: the extravagances, the self-indulgences, the law-breaking, the misjudgements, the lying. The Mail titles led the way in reporting and questioning the flat refurbishment and the Mustique holiday, but they didn't censure him over them. It brushed aside the parties as regrettable, but trivial; critics had lost their sense of perspective, there were more important things to worry about. Well maybe there were, but for all its chanting of the 'he got the big calls right' mantra, it didn't like his government's policies on the key issues of the pandemic lockdown, taxation, or climate change either.

Most wearying of all was the insistence that Johnson was the only person for the job. Even if you accept that he was a 'winner' who saw off the threat of Corbynism and delivered Brexit (that's a very big 'if' for a lot of people), what sort of indictment is it of the 350-odd Conservative MPs that the Mail believes that not one of them is up to leading the team? These are the very people the paper urged its readers to vote into power.

 For the Mail (and others), it is imperative that we have a Conservative government, yet it apparently sees no paradox in simultaneously saying that without this particular man at its head, the party is sunk. No conflict in expecting untainted probity from those of whom it disapproves, while treating honesty and integrity as optional extras in our most senior politician – even after the very ministers he appointed could stomach him no longer. In other words "We want you to vote in this bunch of incompetents whose only asset is their formerly popular, but deeply flawed, captain".

Dropping the captain

Which is exactly what The Times did in 2019, in urging first Tory members and then the country to back Johnson. Once he was in power, though, it published a series of excoriating leaders, attacking him for his policies and his behaviour, finally calling on him to resign. Even the Sun, with its seemingly irrepressible love for Boris and his boosterism, accepted in the end that he should probably go.

But the Mail continued to suffer from the same malaise as the Prime Minister himself, blind to all recent evidence – most notably from the two by-election defeats in June – that it was the very fact that he was at its head that was sinking the party; he was its scourge, not its saviour, and at a time when Keir Starmer was making little headway in building Labour support.

Kill Mordaunt!

After it lost that fight, the paper's double standards with regard to behaviour in public office were even more spectacularly in evidence when it looked as though Penny Mordaunt might claim the crown. Day after day, the Mail titles set out to destroy her chances, finally taking credit for her elimination from the race, saying it would have been a monumental error to let her anywhere near Downing Street. All this was on the basis of Lord Frost accusing her of being workshy, some comments on transgender people, and an unauthorised meeting with the Muslim Council of Britain. In a nutshell, the charge was that she was a lazy liar who broke the rules. Even if she were, the Mail seemed to come a bit late to the notion that these were fatal flaws in a Prime Minister.

Does the Mail truly think the country is in a good place just now, with infrastructure creaking, inflation soaring, the health service on its knees, and trade stalling? We've had a pandemic, there's a war in Europe. But that applies to other countries whose economies are in better shape. It's all very well saying that we should stop being distracted by karaoke parties and let the Prime Minister get on with the job. But we have had 12 years of Conservative government, three of them under Johnson. Maybe it would have been worse under Miliband or Corbyn, but to pretend that Johnson was some new broom coming in to clean up others' mess is disingenuous to say the least.

Meanwhile those lefties on social media have their own theories as to why those titles were so ultra-loyal: Rothermere is a non-dom and Starmer is threatening to review non-dom status; and Labour has also promised to push ahead with Leveson 2, which was supposed to examine the relationships between the press, politicians and the police. In other words, 'Don't think it's the economy, stupid!'

About the contributor

Liz Gerard is a former Night Editor of The Times. She monitors the UK daily national press and reports on it acerbically and in depth for InPublishing fortnightly. A version of this piece first appeared there.

From cronyism to corruption: giving away public money to newspaper friends

Brian Cathcart reveals how Boris Johnson's government channelled millions to mainly wealthy, pro-Tory newspapers in the Covid crisis, secretively, without due process, and, according to one well-placed witness, after proprietors personally rattled their begging bowls at the Prime Minister

In April 2020, barely two weeks into the United Kingdom's first Covid lockdown, Boris Johnson's government introduced a new press subsidy. Though the word 'subsidy' was not used, subsequent statements from the Chancellor, Rishi Sunak, and the Cabinet Office minister, Michael Gove, left no room for doubt on the point. Sunak said the money was being spent 'in support of the print newspaper industry', while Gove said the initiative was 'supporting cherished institutions' (HM Treasury 2020, Society of Editors 2020). The subsidy was a response to intense lobbying by an industry whose advertising revenue had suddenly slumped. Desperate pleas for emergency cash came from the News Media Association (NMA) and the Society of Editors, representing the corporate press, from the Independent and Community News Network (ICNN), representing smaller independent news publishers, and from the National Union of Journalists (NUJ), as Jonathan Haewood, who was involved, has recorded in detail (Haewood 2021). When the new funding was announced the Society of Editors hailed it as 'a vital boost for the industry' (Society of Editors 2020).

All in it together?

It was not exclusively a subsidy. In return for the cash, benefiting publications would participate in a new scheme called 'All In, All Together', providing Covid-related official messages to their readers in the form of advertisements and paid-for editorial content. Soon the national papers and corporately-owned regional and local papers began publishing wraparounds and display advertisements in line with government policies on Covid awareness and containment. Articles also appeared in print and online, more or less signalled as government advertising, telling positive stories about how people were coping and what official support was available. The official timeline of the project shows considerable activity in the first year of the pandemic, reducing thereafter, though articles labelled 'All In, All Together' continued to appear until spring 2022 (Newsworks 2020).

On the surface this may appear worthy but in reality it should be cause for alarm for anyone who cares about journalistic independence, democracy, and the proper use of taxpayers' money. At a time when, as we now know, corruption was at work in government circles, with for example an unlawful 'VIP channel' offering well-connected individuals privileged access to billions in Covid contracts, 'All In, All Together' is evidence of the unhealthy relationship between the Johnson administration and the larger newspaper organisations (BMJ 2022).

'Perceptions of inappropriate interference'

Although there is nothing intrinsically wrong with press subsidies, the Johnson government itself acknowledged as recently as January 2020 that they should be handled with extreme care. In the words of the ministerial response to the Cairncross Review into the future of journalism, 'even an arm's length relationship risks perceptions of inappropriate government interference' (DCMS 2020, par 51). No minister or politician, in other words, should allow so much as a suspicion to arise that they might influence the press through the distribution of public funds. Only three months later, however, Johnson's government was handing public money to the press in a manner that was both selective and secretive.

The vast majority of the cash went to the eight large companies that dominate the NMA (Heawood 2021). These were the national groups – Sun/Times, Mail, Telegraph, Mirror/Express, Guardian and Independent/Evening Standard – plus the regional conglomerates – Reach, Newsquest, and JPI Media. (Reach is also the owner of the Mirror and Express, while JPI Media is now owned by National World.) The hundreds of smaller outfits represented by the Independent Community News Network (ICNN) which had lobbied for help just like the NMA, were in practice cut out of the scheme.

This is open to criticism on several fronts. As small enterprises the

ICNN publishers were more at risk in the Covid crisis than the corporate publishers and therefore in greater need. They are also often innovative and likely to represent the future of news journalism, which should have strengthened their case for assistance. The eight corporations that received the subsidy were long-established businesses generally far better placed to survive the lockdown storm. Four are owned by billionaires, while regional groups Reach and Newsquest had been banking handsome profits for years before the pandemic. JPI Media was so deep in debt it was in trouble with or without Covid.

The prospect of subsidising NMA papers should also have rung alarm bells about political bias. The leading NMA members – the Murdoch, Mail, and Telegraph papers – are highly partisan supporters of Johnson, even personal cheerleaders for him. Johnson had made his reputation as a columnist for the Telegraph, which he was said to have described as his 'real boss', while the closeness of the professional and personal connections between ministers and advisers on the one hand and these papers on the other was probably unprecedented in British history (Cummings 2022a, Bright 2022). Although it is true that 'All In, All Together' money also went to the Guardian and Mirror groups, which have often been critical of the government, the sympathetic papers got the lion's share. The ministerial phrase 'perceptions of inappropriate government interference' is relevant, indeed the scheme carries echoes of the secret government funding of friendly papers practised in the reign of George III.

Official secrecy and proper process?

All In, All Together is also secret: no party to the scheme will say how much it cost the taxpayer or exactly what sums went to which publishers. What we know is that the declared budget for the first three months was £35m and that the scheme ran for almost two years. Neither the Treasury nor the Cabinet Office nor the NMA nor the government's media buying agency OmniGov will say more. Written questions from an MP and a Freedom of Information request also drew blanks (Cathcart, 2022a). A rough external assessment of activity levels over the two years suggests a total bill at least twice and probably three times the initial three-month budget, in other words at least £70m and possibly more than £100m, large sums in press industry terms. Given the free-spending tendencies of the government in this period the final figure could be even higher. The official secrecy surrounding the scheme, moreover, is compounded, and the perception of corruption is increased, by the failure of those organisations that received the cash to fulfil their basic journalistic obligation to scrutinise it for the public benefit.

Another worry is apparent lack of process. All potential public spending should be rigorously tested for fairness, ethical standing, and value for money. Some flexibility was probably justified given the Covid crisis, but this case is conspicuous for the apparent absence of scrutiny. We thus have no official explanation, for example, of how the NMA got to the front of the queue for public funds at a time when almost every industry – entertainment, hospitality, transport and many more – faced unprecedented challenges. We do, however, have one possible glimpse behind the scenes, in the form of a remarkable allegation by Dominic Cummings, who was the senior Downing Street special adviser at the time the subsidy was introduced. In the course of an exchange on Twitter in May 2022 Cummings laid the whole affair at Boris Johnson's door: "also of course the newspapers negotiated direct bungs to themselves with him [Johnson], no officials on calls, then he told officials to send the £- - dressed up as 'covid relief' etc" (Cummings, 2022b). Cummings also asserted that Johnson 'gets direct repeated calls from newspaper *proprietors* not just editors' (Cummings, 2022c).

The picture this conjures up – of newspaper proprietors, presumably including billionaires, exploiting personal access to Johnson to secure funding from the public purse – is alarming, as is the suggestion that civil servants had no involvement beyond disguising the 'bung' as something it wasn't. Downing Street responded to Cummings's tweets without specifically denying any of this, and once again, without declaring how much had been spent. Instead it insisted that 'All In, All Together' had seen "vital public health messaging advertised across approximately 600 titles including UK nationals, regional dailies, weeklies, and independent media. No title received preferred treatment, and all outlets were selected by the government's external media planning and buying agency purely on their ability to engage with audiences at a national, regional and local level" (Cathcart, 2022b).

That requires context. Conveying vital messages to the public is a basic part of the job of the press for which their readers usually pay them, and it is not something for which they should require a special government subsidy. As for those 600 titles, they are overwhelmingly regional and local papers published by large corporations, so the money went into the coffers of Reach, Newsquest, and JPI Media. And finally, while it might be arguable that no title received special treatment, the decision to award the contract to the NMA (among whose members OmniGov divided it) was little different in practice from the corrupt transaction described by Cummings: a prime minister dispensing a cash gift from the public purse to friendly, rich newspaper proprietors.

References

The BMJ (2022) 'Covid-19: Government's use of VIP lane for awarding PPE contracts was unlawful, says judge'. Available at www.bmj.com/content/376/bmj.o96. Accessed 27 July 2022.

Sam Bright (2022) 'Boris Johnson's co-dependent relationship with the right-wing press further exposed' Byline Times 31 January. Available online at bylinetimes.com/2022/01/31/boris-johnson-co-dependent-relationship-with-right-wing-press-further-exposed/ Date accessed 27 July 2022.

Brian Cathcart (2022a) 'Government Refuses to reveal taxpayer cost of secret Covid subsidy for its wealthy press friends', Byline Times, 8 March. Available online at bylinetimes.com/2022/03/08/government-refuses-to-reveal-taxpayer-cost-of-secret-covid-subsidy-for-its-wealthy-press-friends/ Date accessed 27 July 2022.

Brian Cathcart (2022b) 'As Cummings said...' Twitter 12 May twitter.com/BrianCathcart/status/1524683673458651136 Date accessed 27 July 2022.

Dominic Cummings (2022a) '...the real boss...' Twitter 6 June twitter.com/dominic2306/status/1533926055832076289?lang=gu Date accessed 27 July 2022.

Dominic Cummings (2022b) 'also, of course... ' Twitter, 11 May twitter.com/Dominic2306/status/1524394482938093571 Date accessed 27 July 2022.

Dominic Cummings (2022c) '...calls from newspaper *proprietors*...' Twitter, 18 May twitter.com/dominic2306/status/1526836612990177280?lang=en Date accessed 27 July 2022.

Department for Digital, Culture, Media and Sport (DCMS) (2020) 'Government Response to the Cairncross Review'. Available online at www.gov.uk/government/publications/the-cairncross-review-a-sustainable-future-for-journalism/government-response-to-the-cairncross-review-a-sustainable-future-for-journalism. Date accessed 27 July 2022.

Jonathan Heawood (2021) 'All In, All Together? Government subsidy for news', in David Harte and Rachel Matthews (eds) Reappraising Local and Community News in the UK, London, Routledge. Available online at www.taylorfrancis.com/chapters/edit/10.4324/9781003173144-3/together-government-subsidy-news-jonathan-heawood. Date accessed 27 July 2022.

H.M. Treasury (2020) 'VAT scrapped on E-publications', 30 April. Available online at www.gov.uk/government/news/vat-scrapped-on-e-publications Date accessed 27 July 2022.

Newsworks (2022) 'All together – The united news brand campaign to tackle

Covid-19'. Available at www.newsworks.org.uk/all-in-all-together/ Date accessed 27 July 2022.

Society of Editors (2020) '"All in, all together": UK government partners with newspaper industry on Covid-19 ad campaign' 17 April. Available at www.societyofeditors.org/soe_news/all-in-all-together-uk-government-partners-with-newspaper-industry-on-covid-19-ad-campaign/ Date accessed 27 July 2022.

The Times (2020) 'The Times view on the press under coronavirus', 4 April. Available online at www.thetimes.co.uk/article/the-times-view-on-the-press-under-coronavirus-7cvfk36vl Date accessed 28 July 2022

About the contributor

Brian Cathcart started his career at Reuters and was a senior journalist at the Independent papers and the New Statesman before becoming Professor of Journalism at Kingston University London. He was a founder and the first director of Hacked Off, which campaigns for a more ethical press, and he is the author of several books including the award-winning The Case of Stephen Lawrence (Viking,1999). He writes about journalism matters for Byline Times.

ACT FOUR:
IN SICKNESS
AND IN HEALTH

Getting the calls right?

**Andrew Beck sets the scene for assessments
of how Boris Johnson handled public health**

While other Acts in this book explore and evaluate Boris Johnson's career and record in journalism, public life, and politics this Act focuses on his handling of public health in his three years as UK Prime Minister. How did the man with 'unbridled ambition' (Will Walden) handle health? How did someone who appeared to have overlooked that being Government head required him to handle the responsibility of a national health service as well as cope with serious health crises, both inherited and new? How did an administration peopled by politicians just as ambitious as Johnson, and just as inept at doing the job they were assigned in Cabinet, respond to these crises?

This Act starts with a photograph. Jeremy Collins undertakes a very close reading of one image and one event, the UK-hosted UN Climate Change Conference (Cop26), which took place in Glasgow from 31 October to 12 November 2021. The photograph in question featured Boris Johnson flanked by UN secretary General Antonio Guterres and veteran broadcaster and environmentalist Sir David Attenborough. Guterres and Attenborough were both alert and wearing masks, Johnson was apparently asleep and unmasked.

You don't need to be a jobbing semiotician to know that a picture can paint a thousand words but Collins' reading of this image does reveal how the part can stand for the whole (synecdoche), how the one photograph can stand as an index of the broader canvas of the Johnson government's handling of the entire UK pandemic. While some government special advisers might enjoy the benefits of a Media Studies education they are all schooled in the politics of presentation, of what, in an increasingly mediatised political sphere, are now termed the optics. Often to the exclusion of all else, leaving aside all the boosterish pronouncements, the self-promoting rhetoric, they focus on how politicians look. And there could be no doubting that at Cop26 this was not a good look.

Cop26 took place when the UK government was still crazily slaloming from one extreme to another in its efforts to cope with the pandemic. In March 2020 Johnson's response to the first reported cases of Covid-19 was to carry on regardless. Leading by example he went unmasked, he shook hands with everyone he met, he denounced sane voices who argued for lockdown or at least partial restrictions on social interaction. Zigzagging over the formation and implementation of strategies to stem the spread of the virus was clear evidence of bitter debates inside the Johnson government. Although Johnson, if and when he attended key meetings, was presented with scientific advice urging lockdown and, once lockdown was in place, urging caution about the opening up of UK social spaces, this offended his innate libertarianism. Even when he maintained that the UK was open for business ('Hello Covid, you're welcome, do come in'), and even after he was critically ill himself, governmental response was schizophrenic at best.

It's even misleading to talk about the UK government's response to Covid-19 given that the four component countries of the UK all have their own governments, with varying degrees of authority and autonomy, and all adopted sometimes widely divergent approaches to containing the virus' spread, and to managing public health. Johnson didn't seem to be fully aware that he was no longer in England but rather was in Scotland which had maintained a more cautious approach to opening up and the easing of restrictions on social interaction.

The response of Johnson and his key political advisers to the public outcry about the Cop26 photograph was typical of his reaction to any negative press: if you're caught out disobeying the rules, don't change your behaviour, change the rules. Displaying more skill at wriggling around rules than in complying with them Downing Street drew journalists' attention to the conference's updated rules: delegates were now required to wear face-coverings except when sitting down, when eating or drinking, or of they were medically exempt.

From Collins' tight focus on the one image and the one event the camera now pulls out and back to reveal the panoramic view of John Lister on the Johnson government's response to the public health crisis presented by the entire Covid-19 pandemic period. Typical of Johnson's response here is that, while health experts consistently warn that the virus is still very much with us, that nothing should be taken for granted by thinking of the virus in the past tense, in his valedictory address he claimed victory over a vanquished foe. The virus had been defeated and the UK health service was in good shape: 'we protected our NHS. We saved untold thousands and thousands of lives' (Johnson 2022).

John Lister has been reporting and campaigning on public health for nearly forty years. He has consistently tracked moves to reduce the effectiveness of the UK National Health Service whether by attempts to privatise it in whole or part, or by the bogus austerity measures of George Osborne's time as Chancellor of the Exchequer (2010- 2016). Where he often writes in the thick of things here he takes the opportunity to take a longer view and offer an assessment of Johnson's handling of the pandemic. In his typically scrupulously researched contribution he makes astute use of commentary from pro-Conservative newspapers, who could normally be relied on to support a Conservative Prime Minister.

Fair-minded as ever, Lister points out that some things cannot be held against Johnson. Upon assuming the office of Prime Minister he inherited an NHS that was already in a parlous state. Although he could not know that a global pandemic was about to hit the UK he should have known that the NHS had a very low number of intensive care beds, and that its workforce was suffering from an estimated shortfall of 84,000 vacant posts.

What can be held against him is his chaotic and scattershot response to the pandemic. What can also be held against him is a myopic reliance on private sector operators, a chumocracy of pals from school or university days, and a reluctance to formulate and implement strict measures on social movement and international travel. The reliance on the private sector came as manna from heaven for many private hospitals. The UK government-industrial-medical complex revealed itself in the form of NHS England block booking private hospital beds, rescuing many private hospitals from threatened bankruptcy or closure. Never wanting to waste a crisis, for the UK private health sector it was almost business as usual. In a 2021 piece analysing how the Johnson government's handling of the Covid pandemic had affected the NHS Lister concluded that 'private hospitals still get to choose whether to prioritise patients' lives or profits. It could have been so different had wiser decisions been taken' (Lister 2021). Furthermore, the key contracts gifted to private sector operators in the Johnson chumocracy meant that procurement rules were ignored. Boris Johnson made the right calls but to the wrong people. In response to the question 'did Johnson's actions increase the numbers of avoidable deaths?' Lister's grave conclusion is 'The answer is clearly yes'.

Right from March 2020 when Johnson dithered and delayed for 22 days before reluctantly moving to the imposition of some form of lockdown, his government's response was characterised by indecision, screeching U-turns, painfully untrue promises of actions and achievements, failed schemes, and grotesque wastes of public money (the government wrote off £8.7bn on inappropriate or useless PPE alone). In exactly the way that Johnson fudged his lack of compliance with safety protocols at Cop26, he applied the same strategy on a far grander scale at the tardy outset of national measures against the pandemic. By renaming Public Health England the National Institute for Health Protection (under which NHS Test and Trace and the Joint Biosecurity Centre were subsumed), Johnson gave himself and his government a blank cheque of indeterminacy to underwrite their erratic and invariably self-serving measures.

The world has not seen the last of Covid-19. Even its very presence has been either downplayed or decried by the Johnson government's vainglorious claims about its successes. For a more sober view one could point to the conclusion of the 18 July 2022 joint editorial by BMJ and Health Service Journal: 'the government must stop gaslighting the public and be honest about the threat the pandemic still poses to them and the NHS. Being honest with the public will have two positive results, it will encourage the public to modify behaviour and, we hope, provoke urgent reflection about how the NHS is in such a mess so soon after the nation was applauding it on their doorsteps'.

The sad reality of UK politics after twelve years of Conservative administrations is that when MPs are promoted to government posts they seem to ignore the sign on their office door and simply carry on pursuing their own career goals regardless of the job they are meant to be doing. Addressing this phenomenon James Butler concluded that it's 'damaging to be governed by intellectually deficient, personally ambitious, corrupt or simply uninterested politicians. Fewer ministers than ever genuinely care about their departments. They are focused instead on jostling at Westminster and angling for a slot on Question Time' (Butler 2022). However poor their records in handling their government brief the public rhetoric is always that these are the most difficult circumstances in UK if not human history, that they are doing a magnificent job, and that they have never made a false move. The line from Johnson, and from his acolytes who model themselves on him, has always been that Big Dog got the big calls right. Well, though force of circumstance might have driven him to make some of the right calls, his preference was and always remains to make his calls to the wrong people.

References

British Medical Journal/Health Service Journal (2022) 'The health service is not living with Covid, it's dying from it', joint editorial, 18 July.

James Butler (2022) 'Johnson's downfall', London Review of Books, 21 July.

Boris Johnson (2022) 'Boris warns "Remainiacs plotting in dark corners of Westminster" as he hands back No 10 key', Sunday Express, 24 July.

John Lister (2021) 'Short-sighted policies threaten a long-term weakening of the NHS', in John Mair (ed) The Pandemic: A Year of Mistakes?, Goring: Bite-Sized Books.

Will Walden (2022) Loose Ends, BBC Radio 4, 6 August.

The national disgrace and the national treasure

An ostensibly ambiguous photograph of Boris Johnson at the Cop26 climate conference in 2021 generated critical news coverage because it reinforced a popular narrative about him – a self-absorbed egotist – which provided a clear contrast with the public image of David Attenborough. Jeremy Collins offers a close reading of this photograph

Photographs furnish evidence. Something we hear about, but doubt, seems proven when we're shown a photograph of it. In one version of its utility, the camera record incriminates – Susan Sontag, On Photography

Cop26

The UN Climate Change Conference UK 2021 (Cop26) began in Glasgow on 1 November 2021, with the aim of agreeing wide-ranging measures to address the global climate crisis. It was delayed for a year due to the pandemic and, in the run up to the conference, concerns had been raised about the safety of the event due to a steady rise in Covid infections over the summer. By mid-October there were over 40,000 daily cases (Cases in the UK | Coronavirus in the UK, n.d.), and there was a concern that Cop26 would exacerbate the problem, with Professors Linda Bauld and Devi Sridhar (both well-known media experts on the pandemic) suggesting the possibility of a 'Glaswegian spike' in infections (Eden, 2021; Johnson, 2021). The day before the conference began, Scottish First Minister Nicolas Sturgeon issued a request for delegates and other visitors to follow the rules in Scotland by "wearing face coverings in shops, on public transport and in crowded spaces, by testing regularly, and by following the rules within the summit site itself" (Vevers, 2021).

The photograph

It was in this context that Boris Johnson attended the opening ceremony. Sitting with UN Secretary General Antonio Guterres to his right and environmentalist and broadcaster David Attenborough to his left, both of whom were wearing masks, Johnson was photographed unmasked, with his eyes closed, apparently asleep.

The reaction

The reaction to the image, as it circulated on social media and 'legacy' media, was highly critical. Many Twitter users shared the image and criticised Johnson as a 'national disgrace', who 'can't be bothered to wear a mask', and the hashtag #ourpm was trending as one of the most popular on the day mainly in critical response to the image.

Johnson faced a 'backlash for "not caring" about David Attenborough' according to HELLO! magazine. The Guardian noted a clear distinction between Johnson and Attenborough:

On stage and in front of 120 world leaders, the contrast between the two men was striking. The naturalist was sombre and serious. There was a "desperate hope" we might still avoid disaster, Attenborough said in Glasgow, in the most memorable phrase of the week. Joe Biden was among those to give him a standing ovation.

But overall the prime minister appeared to rely on the jokes and verbal antics that have served him well in the past.

Johnson's Cop26 address was met with stony silence. The prime minister left pauses for laughs. They never came (Harding and Walker, 2021).

The image of Johnson in the photograph, maskless and unengaged, was therefore tied in this article to his conference speech, and the wider view of Johnson as unwilling or unable to adopt the serious role of the statesman, relying instead on bluff charm but held in contempt by those present.

Other news items sought to highlight the contrast between the two men. The Independent presented comments from social media 'fans of David Attenborough' who 'expressed outrage':

The Charlatans singer Tim Burgess wrote: 'If you can't bring yourself to wear a mask while sitting next to 95-year-old David Attenborough, how can you say that you actually care about other people? @BorisJohnson you really should be ashamed of yourself.'

Of course the emphasis on Attenborough's age was intended to highlight his vulnerability to the virus. Another fan noted how masks are about protecting others, and that Johnson's carelessness in going maskless, 'especially sat next to a national treasure like Attenborough says it all' (Chilton, 2021). Labour politicians Anna McMorrin and shadow trade minister Bill Esterson weighed in to criticise Johnson, with Esterson quoted as suggesting that the image 'says it all about Johnson' (Sky News, 2021). The Metro referenced Nicola Sturgeon's 'selfie', shared on Twitter, of herself with Attenborough – both masked – in order to make the comparison with Johnson (Jones, 2021).

National treasure, national disgrace

CNN referred to Attenborough as a 'veteran broadcaster and climate campaigner' (CNN, 2021), and the description of him as a 'national treasure' adds an extra element to the 'outrage' over the photograph. Attenborough's over seventy years career making ground-breaking educational TV natural history documentaries, becoming BBC Director of Programmes, and campaigning across a range of conservation, environmental, and climate change issues has established him as an authority commanding a huge amount of respect across the British cultural landscape (e.g. WWF, n.d.). The photograph (along with UN Secretary General Guterres) shows three older white men in suits who are visually similar. The cultural distinction between the hugely admired and respected Attenborough and the divisive figure of Johnson could hardly be greater. Esterson's point that the image was indicative of Johnson's character ('it says it all') underlines the way in which the photograph reinforced a particular view of Johnson: privileged, thoughtless, careless of others, self-absorbed, egotistical.

The 'full story'

No 10 responded by pointing to the updated conference rules which suggested that delegates were required to 'wear a face covering except when seated, eating or drinking or if medically exempt' (BBC News, 2021), and this was reported by a few outlets. Some news organisations also acknowledged that the image did not give 'the whole picture', with the Mirror suggesting that the image 'isn't as straightforward as it seems' (Buchan and Bloom, 2021), and the BBC acknowledging that '[v]iral social media moments often don't tell the full story' (BBC News, 2021). The Huffington Post noted the 'scathing criticism' the image had generated from 'horrified people' before arguing that other images in the same run showed Johnson both alert and wearing a mask, while others showed Attenborough himself without a mask: 'In fact, the only figure in the series who appears to have kept his face covering on throughout is UN secretary general Antonio Guterres' (Nicholson, 2021). These alternative images were circulating in social media as well as being reported on in mainstream outlets; nevertheless, they made little impact on the overall narrative the photograph was thought to convey.

Conclusion: an iconic picture

In the run-up to the conference one news article raising the issue of Covid safety at the event had noted that the rules for running the conference safely were intended to apply to everyone in attendance, while the House of Commons had a two-tier system in which 'staff members and journalists are required to wear masks, but lawmakers aren't' (Kirka, 2021). This subsequently provided fuel for the argument that emerged following the Cop26 photograph of Johnson: it offers a conception of parliamentarians in general, and Johnson in particular, as elites who consider themselves exempt from the rules imposed on others. (Of course this also supported the criticisms of (at the time) alleged parties within Downing Street during lockdown which eventually snowballed into Partygate.) This framing of Johnson resonated to the extent that the 'alternative' images of the same event in which Johnson was masked and Attenborough wasn't simply could not dampen down the 'backlash' that Johnson received. The narrative of Johnson as an egotist, careless of the concerns of others – which carried over from his personal life to his time in journalism and in politics as London mayor, foreign secretary and prime minister – had become dominant to the extent that the idea of the photograph as a potentially misleading instant in the flow of time was ignored. In this case, as Susan Sontag has suggested, the image is offered as evidence of what we already knew: 'A photograph passes for incontrovertible proof that a given thing happened' (Sontag, 2008: 5). At the end of 2021, as newspapers rounded up another tumultuous year, among The Telegraph's 'Iconic Pictures of 2021' the November section began with a powerful image which somehow summarised the Prime Minister: the photograph of Guterres, Johnson, and Attenborough, with the central figure seemingly drowsing, eyes closed, and unmasked (Kelly, 2021).

References

BBC News(2021) 'COP26: Did Boris Johnson and Sir David Attenborough break face mask rules?' 3 November. Available at:

www.bbc.com/news/newsbeat-59149998 (accessed 29 July 2022).

Lizzy Buchan and Dan Bloom (2021) 'Johnson 'sleeping' and maskless claims explained – what the photos actually show' Available at: www.mirror.co.uk/news/politics/boris-johnson-sleeping-maskless-claims-25355118 (accessed 29 July 2022).

Cases in the UK | Coronavirus in the UK (n.d.) Available at: coronavirus.data.gov.uk/details/cases (accessed 6 July 2022).

Louise Chilton (2021) 'David Attenborough fans furious over photo of maskless Boris Johnson next to him' Available at: www.independent.co.uk/artsentertainment/tv/news/ cop26boris-johnson-david-attenborough-b1949702.html (accessed 29 July 2022).

Alicia Lloyd and Ben Kirby (2021) 'Boris Johnson talks up COP26 climate deals but stumbles on Attenborough mask controversy' Available at: www.cnn.com/2021/11/02/uk/boris-johnson-interview-cop-amanpour-climateexclusive-intl-cmd/index.html (accessed 29 July 2022).

Tom Eden (2021) 'Cop26 will see Covid cases spike and may lead to new restrictions, expert warns' Belfast Telegraph, 14 October. Available at: www.belfasttelegraph.co.uk/news/uk/cop26-will-see-covid-cases-spike-and-may-lead to-new-restrictions-expert-warns-40971400.html (accessed 27 July 2022).

Luke Harding and Peter Walker (2021) 'Like a clown': what other countries thought of Boris Johnson at Cop26' The Guardian, 5 November. Available at: www.theguardian.com/environment/2021/nov/05/bit-like-a-clown-boris-johnson-makes-impression-cop26 (accessed 29 July 2022).

HELLO!(2021) 'Boris Johnson faces backlash for 'not caring' about David Attenborough's health at COP26' Available at: www.hellomagazine.com/healthandbeauty/health-and-fitness/20211102125350/boris-johnson-backlash-david-attenborough-health-maskless-cop26/ (accessed 29 July 2022).

Simon Johnson (2021) 'Cop26 summit risks virus spike in central belt' The Telegraph, 14 October. Available at: www.telegraph.co.uk/politics/2021/10/14 (accessed 13 July 2022).

Harrison Jones (2021) 'Fury as Boris Johnson fails to wear mask next to David Attenborough' Metro. Available at: metro.co.uk/2021/11/02/cop26-boris-blasted-for-not-wearing-mask-next-to-david-attenborough-15526838/ (accessed 29 July 2022).

Guy Kelly (2021) 'The iconic pictures of 2021 – a year of angry protests, emotional farewells, famous victories... and more Covid' The Telegraph, 28 December.

Available at: www.telegraph.co.uk/news/2021/12/28/review-2021-iconic-photographs-newsroundup-things-will-get-better/
(accessed 29 July 2022).
Danika Kirka (2021) 'As COVID cases rise, some activists fearful of climate talks'
Available at: apnews.com/article/climate-science-europe-health-environment-and-nature-26dd4a1edbb3bb04a6516d7233451bc6 (accessed 29 July 2022).
Kate Nicholson (2021) 'Why That Photo Of Boris Johnson Without A Mask Next To David Attenborough Isn't The Whole Picture'
Available at:
www.huffingtonpost.co.uk/entry/boris-johnson-david-attenborough-cop26-mask-sleeping-uk-6180fcb3e4b0bf8728dc5bbb
(accessed 8 July 2022).
Sky News(2021) COP26: Boris Johnson faces backlash after being pictured without facemask while next to Sir David Attenborough. Available at: news.sky.com/story/cop26-borisjohnson-faces-backlash-for-failing-to-wear-mask-while-sitting-next-to-sir-david-attenborough-12458494 (accessed 29 July 2022).
Susan Sontag (2008) On Photography, London: Penguin.
Dan Vevers (2021) NIC'S VISITOR MASK PLEA.The Sun, 31 October.
Available at:
www.thesun.co.uk/news/
WWF(n.d.) Sir David Attenborough, OM, CH, CVO, CBE, FRS.
Available at:
www.wwf.org.uk/council-of-ambassadors/sir-david-attenborough
(accessed 29 July 2022).

About the contributor

Dr Jeremy Collins is senior lecturer in Media Studies and the course leader for Film and Television Production BA (Hons) at London Metropolitan University. He has taught modules in media and communications theory and history, communication ethics, promotional media, and research methods, and currently teaches modules in Critical and Contextual Studies for students of film and in the Foundation programme for The Sir John Cass School of Art, Architecture and Design.

Big dog got the big calls wrong

Despite Boris Johnson's claims about his successes in dealing with the Covid-19 pandemic John Lister analyses the government's record and finds he had little to celebrate and much to lament

On 25 July 2022 figures showed that 12,500 NHS beds in England (one in eight) were filled with Covid patients, down from the most recent peak, but almost eighteen times the previous low point of 700 in June 2021. The pandemic is not over, and while vaccinations have limited the severity of the illness for many and significantly reduced the numbers of deaths, there are concerns that continued waves of infection will be a problem for years to come.

Nonetheless all of the precautionary public health measures that were eventually put in place to combat the virus have now been scrapped, despite scientific advice to the contrary, and large numbers of the public remain unvaccinated. Ministers who have defended Boris Johnson's record, and Johnson himself, now talk about the pandemic in the past tense, boasting that despite their partying, and the billions wasted on crony contracts and test and trace, Downing Street got 'all the big calls right'.

That claim is hard to swallow. It has been explicitly challenged by the Mirror, and by Ian Dunt in the i, arguing 'Nothing could be further from the truth', and it has been ridiculed by Robert Shrimsley in the Financial Times, comparing it with arguing: 'I know I just drove the car into a lamppost, but I did sort out the loft conversion. You know, I got the big calls right'.

Even the Sun could be seen visibly falling out of love with Johnson as his authority collapsed in early July, describing him as a 'greased piglet', even while arguing in an editorial that he had 'got the big calls right'.

While Johnson's fan club in the right-wing tabloids (Express, Mail) and of course the Telegraph have largely parroted the same claims, the 'quality' arm of Murdoch press, the Times and Sunday Times, have a more ambiguous position, having carried analysis in 2020 of '38 days when Britain sleepwalked into disaster,' in which: 'Boris Johnson skipped five Cobra meetings on the virus, calls to order protective gear were ignored and scientists' warnings fell on deaf ears. Failings in February may have cost thousands of lives." In May 2020 the Times again flagged up: '22 days of dither and delay on coronavirus that cost thousands of British lives'.

Johnson's health balance sheet

So how are we to evaluate the balance sheet of Johnson's leadership on this crucial issue?

Firstly let's clear away what we can't blame him for. Johnson was clearly not responsible for the pandemic, nor indeed has he ever had responsibility for the NHS, or for the austerity policies imposed in 2010 by Tory Chancellor George Osborne which inflicted real terms cuts on NHS spending for a decade. Austerity forced a continual reduction in front line beds from 2010, leaving the UK as a whole, and England in particular, near the bottom of the league of comparable countries in 2019 for provision of beds, doctors, nurses, and diagnostic scanners, with growing delays in accessing emergency services, and a waiting list of 4.5 million and rising.

So an assessment of Johnson's handling of the Covid-19 pandemic needs to be coupled with an understanding that these pre-existing Tory government failures had left a poorly-resourced, understaffed, inadequately-equipped NHS to deal with the most serious pandemic in a century.

But in taking the Tory leadership in 2019 Johnson effectively embraced and continued the same approach, adding his own vacuous promise of '40 new hospitals' in the autumn of 2019 and in the election manifesto, despite nowhere near enough funding to make it possible.

Johnson insists that his stewardship of the fight against Covid limited the death toll, but experts have warned and concluded otherwise. On the most recent published comparison of excess deaths during the pandemic, based on figures up to 2021, the UK comes out 10th out of 17 countries.

However public health expert Martin McKee points out that comparing excess deaths tends to show countries with high levels of health inequalities and winter mortality (like the UK) in a more favourable light. The Kings Fund, too, notes, 'Excess deaths in the UK from January 2020 to June 2021 were higher than in most West European and high income countries, even though its pre-pandemic life expectancy was lower than in many comparator countries'.

So did Johnson's actions increase the numbers of avoidable deaths? The answer is clearly yes.

Johnson did not really engage with the Covid crisis until the start of March 2020, when Covid cases were already doubling every three to four days. Despite pandemic modelling suggesting the possibility of 200,000 deaths, Johnson refused to impose a lockdown until the end of March, when infections had soared to 1.5 million.

As early as April a detailed Sunday Times report blamed this delay for 'causing many thousands more unnecessary deaths,' and posed sharp questions:

One day there will be an inquiry into the lack of preparations during those 'lost' five weeks from January 24. There will be questions about […] why so little was done to equip the National Health Service for the coming crisis. […] why it took so long to recognise an urgent need for a massive boost in supplies of personal protective equipment (PPE) for health workers; ventilators to treat acute respiratory symptoms; and tests to detect the infection.

The verdict is in

When Johnson's cabinet did respond to the PPE crisis and the need for ventilators, they acted to bypass normal procurement and establish a fast-track 'VIP lane' (subsequently ruled unlawful) that awarded contracts without competition to companies with little, if any relevant expertise, but run by cronies of ministers. Multi-million contracts were handed out without proper technical checks, at inflated prices, many of them supplying goods which proved 'useless to the NHS', wasting £8.7bn – 72% of the total £12.1bn spent.

Tens of billions more were wasted on a shambolic and ineffective privatised test and trace system, run not by public health experts but by another (unlawfully appointed) ministerial crony, Baroness Dido Harding, supported by teams of highly-paid management consultants, and delivered by Serco and other contractors. The Commons' Public Accounts Committee found no clear benefits from the programme, which cost as much as £37bn.

The failure to take testing seriously was most tragically exposed by the heavy toll of 20,000 deaths in care homes in the first wave of the pandemic as NHS hospitals implemented government policy and discharged thousands of patients to social care with no requirement for them to test negative. This policy has since been found to be irrational and unlawful, and Johnson's Health Secretary, Matt Hancock's notorious claim that the government 'threw a protective ring' around the care homes was cruelly disproved.

There was more irresponsibility in the summer of 2020. The 'Eat Out to Help Out' scheme was estimated to have cost £500m but led to two thirds of restaurants and cafes actually losing business, while the scheme increased new Covid-19 infections by between 8% and 17%.

According to the Resolution Foundation, Johnson's further delays in responding to surges in Covid infections in December 2020 led to 27,000 excess deaths. Even the Daily Mail has quoted Sir Jeremy Farrar, a senior member of SAGE and director of the Wellcome Trust charity, stressing the impact of the government errors:

The missteps are clear: the decision on September 21 not to introduce a circuit-breaker; the wait until November before locking down; the premature lifting of lockdown on December 2. These set the scene for what can only be described as the carnage of January and February 2021. The loss of life in that short period dwarfed the first wave in spring last year. Tragedy is too mundane a word to describe what happened: many of these deaths were preventable.

There is also an economic cost to these failures: the Resolution Foundation argues that, because cases were repeatedly allowed to escalate: 'restrictions that were belatedly introduced had to be tighter and last longer to bring the overall case load back down. […] And these tighter restrictions […] in turn have led to the UK experiencing the biggest GDP fall in the G7'.

It's from this much lower level that Johnson now claims that the British economy has been growing faster than others.

In short far from getting the big calls right, repeated failures by Johnson and his ministers to heed the science and take timely precautions have cost thousands of lives, blighted the lives of many thousands more, lined the pockets of hundreds of cronies, and wasted tens of billions of public funds that could have been invested in the NHS. In the words of a joint report by the Commons Health and Science and Technology Committees, Johnson's government's handling of the pandemic has been 'one of the most important public health failures the United Kingdom has ever experienced'.

As the shell-shocked, under-staffed, under-funded NHS tries to claw its way out of the additional chaos caused by the pandemic, health workers may well fear that things could get even worse under his successor: but nobody will be looking back nostalgically to the days of Johnson's premiership.

About the contributor

Dr John Lister has been a health journalist since 1984, and has written books on the NHS, on global health systems, Global Health versus Private Profit (Libri 2013), and on health journalism, First Do No Harm (Libri 2014). His most recent book (with Jacky Davis) is NHS Under Siege: The fight to save it in the age of Covid (Merlin 2022). He is co-founder and co-editor of The Lowdown (lowdownnhs.info).

ENTR' ACTE: CLOWN TIME

Just saying

We have entered an age where reporters, political commentators, and comedians can be completely unfiltered in what they say about politicians. Politicians themselves frequently appear similarly unrestrained. Boris Johnson has not only been the butt of savage humour but has also crafted a public persona as a comic figure. Andrew Beck introduces this comic interlude by looking at the historic precedents for the Boris Johnson three-ring circus as well as the clown himself

Where did it all start? How did we end up in a situation where journalists could say virtually anything about politicians and politicians could say virtually anything about anyone and anything? Examples abound in classical literature of people being rude about public figures and doubtless there are rock paintings depicting thoroughly obscene things happening to tribal leaders. And Jonathan Swift was no slouch at lampooning the foibles of public figures. But in modern times how did we arrive at the situation where journalists, comedians, and citizens could be as grotesquely and obscenely funny about politicians with little or no comeback? How could politicians be as unguarded in what they said about not only their political opponents but also key demographics one would have thought they would have done anything not to alienate? Obviously social media has played a role in helping ordinary people loosen if not take off the gloves to vent their spleens about politicians but how did this kind of talk walk into and camp out in such august mainstream arenas as The Guardian or the BBC? And where does Boris Johnson fit into all of this?

The abandoning of reporters' reverence for politicians seem to go hand-in-hand with the politicians' own shedding of inhibitions and trying their comedic hands. In terms of trying to track down the origins of these phenomena Hunter S Thompson's exhaustive account of the 1972 US Presidential election Fear And Loathing On The Campaign Trail '72 isn't such a shoddy place to start. This anything-goes approach to covering politicians is sometimes characterised as a key component of the New Journalism. Thompson might just have arrived at this gloves-off approach to political reporting due to his own idealism or naiveté about the political process. Certainly he had little experience covering US politics until his harrowing experience at the 1968 Democratic Convention in Chicago closely followed by his own 1970 Freak Power candidacy for sheriff in Aspen, CO.

Richard Nixon 1972

What is undeniable is the sheer savage comic invention Thompson brought to describing politicians. Here's one example from Fear and Loathing On The Campaign Trail '72. Beneath a drawing of then-US President Richard M Nixon in Nazi regalia Thompson wrote: 'Little is known of this picture except that Mr. Nixon (center) suffered from a power complex, a hatred of humanity, near impotence and finally premature senility which resembled Parkinson's disease – or an advanced stage of neuro-syphilis caught during his student days – which has hallucinatory effects on the victim giving him a sense of grandeur. The second possibility has been ruled out on the grounds that at the time Mr. Nixon was a student it would have been socially impossible for him to contract the disease except from a lavatory seat. He died senile in an anti-environment bunker near Camp David, seated before a sun-ray lamp in a deckchair wearing only a pair of old style "jackboots"' (Thompson 1973).

Boris Johnson 2022

In his time as UK Prime Minister Boris Johnson seems to have brought out the best (or the worst: you chose) in British journalists and comedians, especially so in his final days in office. Marina Hyde brings a remarkable combination of astute political commentary, the capacity to wind in popular cultural allusions, a delight in scatological verbal invention, and a Theatre of the Absurd sensibility to her Guardian columns. Just after Johnson announced his grudging resignation from the highest political office in the UK she offered her reflections on this spectacle: 'Boris

Johnson is leaving office with the same dignity he brought to it: none. I've seen more elegant prolapses. Having spent 36 hours on the run from what other people know as consequences, Downing Street's Raoul Moat was finally smoked out of his storm drain on Thursday, having awoken that morning with what one aide described portentously as a "moment of clarity"' (Hyde 2022).

Soon after Johnson had this moment of clarity novelist and columnist Edward Docx published 'The Death of Boris the Clown', a fable charting key moments in his public life, perfectly fitting for such a fabulist. Those key moments included: 'His breakthrough show, "Mayor", opened in 2008 and ran for eight exhilarating years'. This was followed by Brexit: 'Like many of the greatest clowns, "Boris" was also the perfect ambassador of meaninglessness. After 'Mayor' came his widely celebrated follow-up 'Brexit: The Referendum' (2016) – which he famously took on tour and which signalled his career-long thematic obsession with making fatuousness festive'. Then came 'Foreign Secretary': 'his first international hit. His instigating moment of bravura was to create a character who was casually xenophobic. While purporting to 'promote British interests' abroad, he would continually stage the precise opposite'. From here he moved on to the 'problem' of Brexit: 'since the imaginary 'problem' had been mostly summoned up by his invention, it stood to reason that only he could fix it. In other words, Brexit' would only 'get done' if the public bought tickets to see his new show: 'Brexit 2: Prime Minister'. This is a far more elaborate production in the Johnson Show: 'Prime Minister' also had the largest cast of supporting clowns he had ever used. Those he called 'ethics advisers' were custard-pied one after another as they came by on a merry-go-round featuring characters from Peppa Pig'. Finally it all goes wrong, the masquerade is over, and the audience sees the tears of the clown: 'The final moments of the clown combined a kind of diminishing demonic purposelessness with a gigantic morbidity. At the last, "Boris" stood alone, berating a vanishing audience for their ingratitude and shouting betrayal at the low rag-and-bone sky' (all Docx 2022).

Eight days after Docx's piece was published comedian Frankie Boyle appeared on Channel 4's topical satirical programme The Last Leg. Warming his hands at the bonfire of Johnson's vanities Boyle turned his withering eye on the contenders for Johnson's crown. How would his successor be chosen, and who were the final two contestants? 'We're going to have the next Prime Minister chosen by a very small group of elderly people during a heatwave and it's going to be either Rishi Sunak, a guy whose greatest desire in life is to be pegged by Thatcher's ghost, or Liz Truss, who would be the first Prime Minister to forget to breathe and just die' (Boyle 2022).

Johnson as comic

Humour comes in many varieties: it can work by recognition, by fear (usually of the Other), by exaggeration, as insult, as caricature, or as grotesquery. Varieties and variations are endless. But it is difficult to understand Boris Johnson's reputation as an adult comic given that his humour appears to be frozen in his boyhood or, more accurately, his days as a schoolboy.

Johnson's humour hasn't moved on from the sixth form debating society. It is characterised by petty insults, sometimes characterised by verbal ingenuity and invention, but more often simply name-calling. His name-calling of Keir Starmer as Captain Hindsight simply doesn't work because it was neither logical nor true. Hindsight means getting the calls right from a future perspective, that is, by cheating. It is bogus prediction, rewriting history after the fact. Given that Starmer was frequently proven right by events as they unfolded a more accurate sobriquet for Starmer would have been Captain Foresight.

The sense that Johnson was never far away from the school quadrangle or even the nursery was evidenced in former 10 Downing Street aide Cleo Watson's memories of her time there: 'My role at No 10 sounds fancy, but a lot of the time I was much closer to being Boris's nanny. At the start of the pandemic, testing was limited so, like everyone else, the PM regularly had his temperature taken to check for symptoms. This was generally done by me, towering over him (with or without heels – I generally found it useful to be physically intimidating in the role of nanny), one hand on a hip, teapot-style, and the other brandishing an oral digital thermometer. 'It's that time again, Prime Minister!' I'd say. Each time, never willing to miss a good slapstick opportunity, he dutifully feigned bending over' (Watson 2022). At the height of the pandemic she even had to scold him for 'making gags such as 'Kung-Flu' and 'Aye! Corona!' (ibid).

Just saying

The evidence that Johnson is lazy is incontrovertible: he's never worked at writing, public speaking, or relationships. He simply grabs what's to hand and makes the best fist of it he possibly can. Enabled by a lowering of standards of public discourse where anything can be and is said, he acts on the principle that if people take offence his excuse is that it was just bants. Getting your excuse in first as a pre-emptive strike has become a lazy trope whereby you say something unconscionable and then quickly say or write 'Just saying'.

That name-calling is redolent of the prefects' common room, as are his social attitudes, especially towards women and gay men. Fundamentally he thinks women are for shagging, and gay men are funny. Gay men are 'tank-topped bumboys'. Lesbians don't seem to exist in the Johnsonverse, unless, that is, as he might put it, wanting to flaunt his Classics degree and his mastery of schoolboy smut, as skinmag images of sapphic sisters supplying spaffing stimulus.

But where is the clown? Send in the clown
Don't bother he's here

This comic interlude in the book is all about Johnson and humour. Who better to analyse Johnson's comic reputation than Oliver Double? Initially taking his own experience as a working stand-up comedian Double then began researching the work of other comedians and has been writing about comedy since the 1990s. He joined the University of Kent in 1999, and is now Reader in Drama and Theatre, Head of Comedy and Popular Performance, and still an occasional performer. Given that so many public and private commentators have seriously characterised Boris Johnson as funny we thought it would be a good idea to ask him to evaluate Johnson as a stand-up comedian. Beginning with Johnson's April 1998 first appearance on the BBC's Have I Got News For You programme Double finds him 'more pisstaken than pisstaking'. Exploring the creation, cultivation, and honing of his comic schtick Double finds him not so funny at all, indeed, at times he appears simply incoherent. But we leave the last word here to the man himself. In the 24 July edition of the Sunday Express Johnson itemised his achievements in his three years as UK Prime Minister. It is simply beyond satire.

References

Frankie Boyle (2022) The Last Leg, Channel 4, Open Mike Productions, 22 July.
Edward Docx (2022) 'The Death of Boris the Clown', New Statesman, 13 July 2022
Marina Hyde (2022) 'The good news: Johnson's on the way out. The bad news: look who's on the way in', The Guardian, 9 July.
Hunter S Thompson (1973) Fear And Loathing On The Campaign Trail '72, San Francisco: Straight Arrow Books.
Cleo Watson (2022) 'Karma has returned with interest', Tatler, September.

'Incapable of proper action': Boris Johnson as stand-up comedian

Boris Johnson has developed a stand-up persona to get laughs and provide cover for his failings. Oliver Double examines how in the Covid era the joke started to pall. Compared with real comedians, he's not all that funny

Boris Johnson's appearances on Have I Got News for You have passed into legend as a comic triumph. Not only did they bag him a BAFTA nomination for Best Entertainment Performance in 2004, but many believe they paved his way to becoming Mayor of London and, eventually, Prime Minister. In this light, looking back at his first appearance in April 1998 – almost a quarter-century on – the comparative lack of laughs he got on that occasion is somewhat surprising. For the first twenty minutes or so, he's more piss-taken than piss-taking, his own interjections little more than set-ups for Paul Merton's and Ian Hislop's punchlines. He only starts getting big laughs when Hislop grills him about his fraudster chum Darius Guppy 'ringing you up on tape and suggesting that you help him beat up a journalist who was looking into him'. Johnson grins like a boy caught raiding the school tuckshop, and replies, 'That did come up', earning him three seconds of full-throated laughter.

Since coming to public prominence, I've always seen Johnson as more stand-up comedian than clown, with a well-worked persona that appeals to audiences and shields him from criticism. The seminal alternative comedian Tony Allen theorised that performing to a live audience 'appears to trigger a sort of strategic identity crisis', in which 'various sides of our personality come to our assistance' and recommends that, 'However idiosyncratic or inappropriate these minority personalities appear to be, they should all be given an audition' (Allen, 2002: 35). Something like this seems to be happening here, with Johnson auditioning his insouciant, childish, roguish side and finding it works for him. As Sophie Quirk wrote, 'The persona is clearly manipulative in that it is a skilful presentation of the performer's personality that controls perception in order to direct the audience's interpretation and facilitate the gag' (Quirk, 2015: 131). Clearly, the line 'That did come up' would be unfunny – and possibly appalling – without Johnson's now-familiar naughty-boy persona facilitating the gag.

'Totally stitched up'

Still, Johnson was unhappy that he had been, as he put it, 'totally stitched up', and wrote a piece for The Spectator (later reprinted in the Mirror) revealing the backstage practices of HIGNFY. He feigned outrage that they were shown the questions two hours before filming, that they 'were allowed back to our dressing rooms to collude', and that Hislop and Paul Merton had notes – 'pages of stuff' – in front of them (1998). Johnson isn't alone in being surprised at the reality of how comic performance works. As I've previously argued, 'The paradox of live comedy is that while it may look effortless and spontaneous, that spontaneity has been won through hard work' (Double, 2020: 86). Despite appearances, comedians work tirelessly, generating and constantly refining their material, using audience responses to make it more and more efficient at getting laughs. As Bridget Christie puts it, 'Everything is always a work in progress' (in Williams 2016).

It's not surprising that Johnson would be flabbergasted to find that anybody works hard at anything, but he seems to have learned from his experiences on HIGNFY, perhaps by observing the comedians he appeared with over the years – not just Merton, but also guest panellists like Shazia Mirza, Stephen K Amos, and Sue Perkins. He has certainly honed his persona. In his debut performance his hair was comparatively kempt, but the next time he appeared in December 1999 it was more like the trademark explosion-in-a-haystack hairstyle that we know today. Just as Milton Jones' madly messed-up hair provides a visual context for his surrealism, and Paul Foot's ostentatious mullet advertises his eccentricity, Johnson's crazy blond thatch helps to establish him as an amiable bumbler, forever getting himself into scrapes through no fault of his own – and being comically nonchalant when caught out. He clearly realises the importance of what John Crace of The Guardian calls his 'toddler hair-cut', because multiple witnesses have seen him carefully messing it up in preparation for TV appearances.

Set list

He has also mastered the stand-up's trick of fooling audiences into think-ing that carefully honed material is just coming off the top of his head.

Ellen DeGeneres acknowledged that, 'Some people have no idea that you do this over and over again. They really think it's something that is brand new' (in Ajaye 2002: 98). Jeremy Vine fell into that trap with Johnson, writing a piece for The Spectator in which he described seeing him giving a speech at an awards ceremony in 2006. Johnson turned up late, having apparently forgotten he was supposed to be speaking. Cadging a piece of paper and a pen, he quickly scribbled down some words. Vine could only make out a couple of them: 'SHEEP' and 'SHARK'. What Johnson was doing would be familiar to any comedian: writing a set list. We have scores of these in the British Stand-Up Comedy Archive at the University of Kent: scribbled-down lists of single words or short phrases indicating the running order of the gags or routines to be performed.

Vine recalls Johnson pretending to have forgotten the name of the awards ceremony, then going from a tall tale about the sheep on his uncle's farm to a routine about his political hero being the Mayor from Jaws – because even though 'some small children were eaten by a shark', the majority got so much pleasure from the beaches remaining open – and finishing with an anecdote about George Brown but apparently forgetting the punchline. All of this provoked uproarious laughter. Vine was amazed at the way Johnson could mine comedy gold from his slapdash approach.

He was even more amazed to see him repeat the same trick eighteen months later at a different awards ceremony – late arrival, feigned surprise that he was due to speak, the palaver with the set list, and exactly the same material – down to the 'forgotten' punchline to the George Brown story.

Comic licence

Why would lacking any sense of preparedness – not to mention a moral compass – be so appealing to audiences? Lawrence E Mintz wrote about the comedian's 'traditional license for deviate behaviour and expression' and described how it worked: "Traditionally, the comedian is defective in some way, but his natural weaknesses generate pity, and more important, exemption from the expectation of normal behavior [...] Because he is physically and mentally incapable of proper action, we forgive and even bless his 'mistakes'" (Mintz, 1985: 74). This description couldn't fit Johnson more perfectly. Playing on being a bumbling rogue made him likeable and hilarious, getting him laughs for forgetting a punchline, or even a much more egregious 'mistake' like cheerfully confessing to being implicated in a plot to have somebody beaten up.

Of course, comic licence isn't infinite, and comedians who behave abysmally in their private life can find them losing a sizeable chunk of their audience. Louis C.K.'s endless jokes about masturbation became less funny once his abusive backstage treatment of female comedians came to light. According to Dominic Cummings, Johnson regularly wheeled out his old Mayor-from-Jaws shtick in meetings where his government's pandemic response was being planned. Given their woeful handling of Covid and the UK's high death rate, joking about keeping the beaches open in spite of children getting eaten is neither funny nor charming. Is it any wonder that by February 2022 his disapproval rating had rocketed to 71 per cent?

'I'm not following this thing particularly closely'

Yet although Johnson developed the skills of a stand-up comedian – and wielded them deftly for a time – we shouldn't overestimate his supposed comic genius. Compared with real stand-ups, his ability to get laughs is a bit hit-and-miss. Perhaps he's just too lazy to put in the hard slog necessary to perfect his technique. In his 2019 Tory conference speech, he fluffed a line about sending Jeremy Corbyn into orbit – accidentally referring to his adversary as 'Jeremy Corbit' – and it got only quiet laughter, isolated cheers, and applause that sounded wearily dutiful.

Similarly, although he had his moments in his final Prime Minister's Questions on 20 July 2022, these were matched by damp squibs. When Keir Starmer asked him why Tory leadership candidates had pulled out of the previous night's televised debate, Johnson started well by pulling out the old comedy insouciance: 'I'm not following this thing particularly closely, but my – [laughter]'. However, things fell apart when he followed this with a joke about the talent of his would-be successors: 'any one of which w- as I say before, like some household detergent, would wipe the floor – er, with [approving hubbub] er with, with, with a, with a, with er, ruh.'

Playing on the literal and colloquial meanings of 'wipe the floor with' is a hoary old gag. Max Miller told a version at the Holborn Empire as long ago as 1938. The fact that this gets a mere hubbub rather than actual laughter isn't surprising given how badly he delivers it, stumbling his way through without so much as completing the sentence, and ending with something which sounds more like the sort of thing Scooby Doo would say than an actual word.

No Volodymyr Zelenskyy

It's not unknown for comedians to go into politics. Johnson's would-be best buddy Volodymyr Zelenskyy springs to mind. However, the gulf between the two of them couldn't be bigger. Whereas Zelenskyy responded to Putin's invasion by accepting the grave responsibility of becoming a heroic wartime leader, Johnson clearly thinks he should have been able to retain the cheerful irresponsibility of the comedian even while running a country. In the age of Brexit, Covid, and the cost of living crisis, this simply wasn't good enough.

References

Franklin Ajaye (2002) Comic Insights: The Art of Stand-up Comedy, Los Angeles: Silman-James Press.

Tony Allen (2002) Attitude: Wanna Make Something of It?, Glastonbury: Gothic Image.

Oliver Double (2020) 'If You Laugh at Something, Then I'll Potentially Keep it': The Praxis of Live Comedy', in Louise Peacock (ed) A Cultural History of Comedy in the Modern Age, London: Bloomsbury pp. 63-86.

Boris Johnson (1998) 'Have I Got News for You: The Show's a Total Fraud', Daily Mirror, 6 May.

Lawrence E Mintz (1985) 'Standup Comedy as Social and Cultural Mediation', American Quarterly, Vol. 37, No. 1 pp. 71-80.

Sophie Quirk (2015) Why Stand-Up Matters, London: Bloomsbury.

Jeremy Vine (2019) 'My Boris Johnson story', The Spectator, 17 June.

Ben Williams (2017) 'How Bridget Christie found the funny side of Brexit', The Guardian, 3 February.

About the contributor

Dr Oliver Double is Reader in Drama at the University of Kent. His books include Stand-Up! On Being a Comedian (1997), Getting the Joke: The Inner Workings of Stand-Up Comedy (2005, 2014), Britain had Talent: A History of Variety Theatre (2012), and Alternative Comedy: 1979 and the Reinvention of British Stand-Up (2020). Before becoming an academic he was a professional comedian on the British comedy circuit, and continues to perform today, albeit as more of a hobby. In 2013, he founded the British Stand-Up Comedy Archive at the University of Kent.

Beyond
satire

**Never someone to seriously break sweat working at
anything, and never someone to fail to use the same
script more than once, in his last days as PM
Boris Johnson maintained the habit of a lifetime.
As closing time sounded on his occupancy of No 10
Downing Street his need to write his own legacy before
more objective assessments were offered was tempered
by his inability to stretch himself and craft
new forms of words for three different audiences.
So it was that virtually the same script was used three
times: firstly, in his 18 July appearance in the House of
Commons; secondly, as a No 10 press statement issued
on 21 July; and thirdly, as an article entitled
'Boris warns 'Remainiacs plotting in dark corners
of Westminster' as he hands back No 10 key'
published in the Sunday Express on July 24.
We leave it to the reader to make of this what they will**

W hen I became Prime Minister three years ago today, the British people were despairing of a deadlocked Parliament, a paralysed Government, and a political system that appeared to be rigged against vast swathes of the country.

The task before me was very clear: to break the logjam and get Brexit done so that we could get on with the vital task of levelling up the United Kingdom. And that's what I did. Hitting the reset button on Parliament by winning the biggest Conservative majority for a generation and, within weeks, extracting our country from the clutches of the European Union.

We took back control of our money.

We took back control of our borders and installed a points based system for immigration.

We took back control of our laws.

And we took back the sovereign right of the British people to determine their own future in Parliament

The Remainiacs and Remoaners and Rejoiners didn't like it then and they don't like it now.

You don't have to look hard to spot them.

Some quietly plotting in dark corners of Westminster.

Others spewing hashtags across social media as they sneer at readers of the Sunday Express and many millions of Brits with whom they disagree.

Still more camped outside Downing Street, bellowing through megaphones at bemused tourists and long-suffering police officers.

But the British people put their faith in me to get the job done.

And as I prepare to leave this fantastic job after three years at No 10 I'm proud to say that's exactly what I did, with Brexit and so much more besides.

Because this government has fought some of the hardest yards in modern political history.

We have had to take some of the bleakest decisions since the war.

And time and again we got the big calls right.

So we can look to the future with a rock-like confidence in what this government has done.

We've invested in our children's futures, giving schools their biggest financial boost for a decade.

We've invested in our precious National Health Service, with a record-breaking increase in funding and around 30,000 extra nurses recruited.

We've invested in making our streets safer, well on track to hit our target of 20,000 new police officers on the beat by the end of next year.

We've invested in making our planet cleaner, with wind farms sprouting like so many giant aquatic daffodils across the vast reaches of the North and Celtic Seas.

We've even invested in making your wi-fi quicker. When I became Prime Minister just nine per cent of British properties could access the fastest gigabit-capable broadband. You know what that number is today? Sixty-eight per cent.

And all this of course against the backdrop of the worst global pandemic in living memory.

Severe Acute Respiratory Syndrome Coronavirus Two. A virus the origins of which we still do not fully understand, the spread of which was appallingly difficult to manage, and the impact of which was simply devastating.

But even in the face of this microscopic yet deadly foe, even as the world was struck with wave after wave, variant after variant the people of this magnificent country did not give up.

And thanks to the courage of the British people and to their indomitable resilience, we protected our NHS. We saved untold thousands and thousands of lives.

And relief, when it finally arrived, came thanks to the genius of British scientists who performed a kind of biological jiu-jitsu, turning the virus on itself in the form of a vaccine from an idea that was pioneered in this country by Edward Jenner in 1796.

A vaccine that, thanks to this government, was safely yet swiftly licensed faster than any in history, and rolled out faster than was the case in any comparable country – helping us get out of lockdown quicker and get our economy growing sooner.

So as I mark three years as Prime Minister it is with immense satisfaction in the work this government has done.

And it is round-the-clock, seven-days-a-week work that continues to this day and will continue until the famous black door closes behind me for the final time.

We're rising to the challenge of rising prices, with £37 billion of help for households. We're giving every family £400, with £1,200 for the most vulnerable. The payments started landing in bank accounts last week – shortly after the single biggest tax cut in a decade started showing up on your payslips.

And of course we are standing, in resolute kinship, with the government and people of Ukraine.

There are some who speculate that today I am more popular in Kyiv than I am in Kensington.

I don't know if that's true but if it is the case then it's not because of what the political commentators say, or what the keyboard warriors of Twitter are up to.

It's because of the foresight and boldness of the government that I lead.

While others dithered and worried about what antagonising Putin would mean for their own prospects, the UK despatched plane after plane loaded with weapons to the Ukrainian front lines.

It was a decision made possible by the biggest investment in defence since the cold war. And a decision that made a tide-turning difference in those crucial first few days as the fiercely brave Ukrainian forces repelled wave after wave of Russian tanks.

The battle for Ukraine is far from over, but I do believe that in time President Zelenskyy and his people will emerge victorious.

And though that victory may be of massive strategic importance in the face of Putin's aggression and adventurism, it will be also a victory of right over wrong.

Of the little guy over the big bully.

That's what this government has always been about. We don't take the easy route, we don't default to standing with the loudest, or the strongest.

For three years we have been sticking up for you. Fighting for what's right. Making this the kind of proud and prosperous country you want it to be.

On the day I arrived at No 10 I made the point that no one had ever succeeded in betting against the pluck and nerve and ambition of this country as we set out into the world.

Much has changed in the intervening three years.

But that's one thing that's as true today as it has ever been.

Boris Johnson was UK Prime Minister from July 2019 to September 2022.

ACT FIVE: TRUMP AND JOHNSON

John Mair introduces the commentators assessing the outbreak of populism on both sides of the Atlantic and the uncanny similarities between Boris Johnson and Donald Trump

Populism is like a bad rash. It has broken out all over the world, usually in right-wing versions such as are found in India and Hungary. In the UK we have had three years of Boris' populism. His primary vehicle was Brexit from the EU and 'Getting Brexit Done!' Johnson rode to power on this populist bus, even one with a lie on the side of it. After the 2016 Brexit Referendum Johnson, the born-again Leaver, has used anti-European sentiment ruthlessly to curry favour with the electorate.

Since knifing Theresa May in the back and becoming 'World King' in 2019, the Boris bandwagon has somewhat been delayed by two years of the Covid pandemic and the war in Ukraine. But his populist sentiments came out soon after the pandemic 'ended' in his attempt in November 2021 to save the parliamentary career of bribe-taker Owen Paterson. That failed dismally. Since then, it has been all downhill for Boris. 'Partygate' exploded in a series of revelatory bombs. Right-wing 'red meat' was regularly thrown by him or his acolytes to help the nation to 'move on' (save his career) but they were lost in a tsunami of lies. Just like with The Donald.

If Trump were a Mastermind subject then David Cay Johnston would be the clear winner. He has spent quarter of a century journalistically ghosting Trump and his nefarious business and political dealings. If Trump slipped up, Johnston was there to dig the knife in. Here the Pulitzer Prize winner excoriates both of them singly and together.

Here he is on Johnson: 'Johnson was famously dismissive of Brexit before becoming its champion, a fluidity that washes away principles is a fundamental element of faux-populist leadership'.

And here he is on Johnson and Trump: 'That either of these children dwelling in adult bodies rose to any position higher than dog catcher should vex us. Their rise shows how the new populism has diverted us from the long human struggle to replace tyrannical monarchs, warlords, and religious zealots'.

Boris was born in the USA and bases much of his schtick on Donald Trump's. The two are peas in a populist pod: 'Think about Johnson cynically saying, 'there are no disasters, only opportunities. And, indeed, opportunities for fresh disasters', and Trump invoking the royal we at every rally to proclaim, 'we love you'.'

Trump revelled in saying and doing anything to please 'his' people in the flyover states. Racism, misogyny, and authoritarianism were all tools in his playbook, as was lying when he disputed (to this day) the clear result of the 2020 US Presidential election, even to the extent of encouraging the Capitol riot on 6 January 2021. Trump, with family and business links to the UK, views Boris as a fellow anti-establishment soul. He called him 'Britain Trump' (English was never the Donald's strongest suit). Both 'Britain Trump' and 'USA Trump' are out in the cold. For now.

Journalist Angela Antetomaso has experience of populism on both sides of the Atlantic. She was an unwilling witness to the explosion of xenophobia in Britain: she was once shouted at on a London bus during the Referendum campaign for being Italian. She moved to New York where she witnessed the last days of the Trump presidency. There Boris was a hero and a character to like for many including the Trumpies: 'Likening Johnson to then-US-President Donald Trump wasn't that hard, after all. The blonde hair, the narcissistic behaviour, the twisted fabrications, the silly jokes, and the at-times-senseless mumbling were too easy a comparison to make'.

She fell in love with his image and fell out again. Neither Boris' lying and its unravelling nor the UK furore about 'Partygate' ever quite successfully crossed the Atlantic so his fall in July 2022 came as a surprise in New York City: 'The petty little lies he churned out almost daily in order to keep himself afloat were too domestic to be exported, and too intricate to be fully explained to foreigners who are not familiar enough with British politics'.

All the same Antetomaso ends her essay with a message of hope: 'The British people, unlike their former PM, do have a moral compass, and it is not going to be easy for Boris Johnson and his chums to ever be trusted again'.

Enjoy their writing.

Peas in a pod:
Donald J Trump
and Boris Johnson

How did two men, both born in New York City, grow up to become the badly misinformed, gratuitously cruel, and incompetent leaders of Britain and the United States? David Cay Johnston asks how could the clowns Boris Johnson and Donald Trump succeed over many worthy competitors, all deeply informed, caring, and well prepared to lead their national governments?

Welcome to the 21st century, where democracy has become a game to the delight of many among the rich.

Many citizens care less about their duties to the body politic, which enables tomfoolery, than soccer fouls and contested baseball pitches.

That either of these children dwelling in adult bodies rose to any position higher than dog catcher should vex us. Their rise shows how the new populism has diverted us from the long human struggle to replace tyrannical monarchs, warlords, and religious zealots. We must never lose focus on choosing serious leaders who promote the general welfare, ennobling the human species to become all that we can be.

Unlike the disputed sports play, the stakes here determine jobs and income, social stability, and the long and far from complete march to expand British human rights and American civil rights. (The difference is that post-war British and European rights draw on human dignity, while American civil rights are rooted in eighteenth-century property law.)

Who are they?

Let's first address who these men tell us they are:

Johnson once wrote in The Spectator: 'The modern British male is useless. If he is blue collar, he is likely to be drunk, criminal, aimless, feckless, and hopeless' while white collar men are only 'slightly better'. At least he made that denigrating observation three years before the 1998 Human Rights Act required all authorities to treat everyone with dignity, fairness, and respect. But in his 2002 book Friends, Voters, Countrymen, Henley's MP stated, 'If gay marriage was OK […] I saw no reason in principle why a union should not be consecrated between three men, as well as two men, or indeed three men and a dog'. And two years after that, while serving as shadow arts minister, he offered up antisemitism, racist slurs, and a crude description of a bosomy woman in his novel Seventy-Two Virgins. At least Johnson can write a compelling piece. His semi-illiterate American counterpart Donald J Trump relied on others to craft his self-aggrandizing books filled with tales of cheating investors, business partners, and employees as well as taking mulligans galore while reporting par for the course.

Trump was even more disrespectful than Johnson when discussing people unlike himself. Trump called Mexicans rapists and murders in 2015, described violent American neo-Nazis as 'very fine people' in 2017, and often urged supporters to violently assault anyone who didn't share their adoration of the con artist extraordinaire.

Hoping to avoid becoming a certified loser on January 6, 2021, Trump incited the first siege of the American Capitol since British soldiers burned it in 1814.

At least, unlike Trump, Johnson doesn't encourage people to think he is a god.

The rise and rise of the clowns

So how did these clowns rise to power? When I attended college in California and the Midwest in the 1960s and 1970s, the prevailing theme of American history courses was that the aristocratic class in British Colonial America created the new nation. Democracy wasn't the product of colonial rabble, most of them barely literate farmers, but rich white men who knew ancient Greek and Roman history.

What brought Johnson and Trump men to power were atrophying political systems decoupled from the interests of all but the thin and super-rich slice of people who finance politicians.

In return for donations, the corporate rich scoop up government benefits by the billions. That, in turn, enhances their influencing campaign donations, reinforcing the vicious, anti-democratic nature of modern politics in Britain and the United States. This unfortunate development is particularly advanced in the United States, where the

Supreme Court pretty much legalised bribing politicians, adopting a wink-and-nod jurisprudence of anything goes between favour seekers and government officials just so long as they don't expressly declare a quid pro quo.

Voters as renters/squatters

What infects British and American politics is a curable problem that those with the most influence prefer to make worse. The problem: millions of eligible voters act like renters or, worse, squatters rather than as what they are: the owners of the British and American governments. The solution is to empower people to understand that they are owners and that they must exercise their ownership rights to further their interests.

It's so easy to dismiss politics as dirty and unworthy. It's hard to understand the complex issues in our modern world, especially in America where more than half of adults read at or below that of a eleven or twelve-year-old child.

To understand the rise of politicians like Johnson, and the pseudo-politician Trump, we must look at who and what is behind the resurrection of populism.

What is so popular about populism?

In theory, populism is an appeal to the vast majority rooted in the idea that economic, political, and social elites run society in their own interests and to the detriment of the ordinary person. American populism began as a late nineteenth-century movement against the exploitation of Midwest farmers by price-gouging freight railroads and the Wall Street tycoons who financed them. Populism has always been tinged with ignorance, as in 'what would a bunch of people dumb enough to be farmers possibly know about how to run a government?' Populism has always been exploited by rich and powerful people who claim to represent ordinary people while working against their interests.

Sociologist Isaac William Martin explained this in his brilliant 2018 book Rich People's Movements. The modern Tea Party, which helped give rise to Trump, grew from decades of efforts by American oligarchs to de-tax themselves. They hired political con artists who sold the hoi polloi on policies damaging their well-being. They relied on cranks, rogues, and a few scholars to polish the most effective ideological marketing pitches. Their goal was to sell the notion that if the rich bear less of the burden of government, all of us will somehow end up better off. Millions of people with little or no savings and punishing debts bought this malarkey just as many working-class Brits were tricked into believing that Brexit would be good for their personal economics.

Johnson was famously dismissive of Brexit before becoming its champion. A fluidity that washes away principles is a fundamental element of faux-populist leadership.

No principles but power

How could such misinformation possibly thrive in what has been called the Information Age? And what of the rhetoric about the wisdom of crowds, an idea heavily promoted by the stunningly profitable high-tech industries that favour libertarianism and anti-government slogans even as they feed off the taxpayer investments that delivered us from the limitations of the Analogue Age and into the ubiquitous Digital Age of the Internet?

How real people think

The answer to those and many other questions lies in how human beings naturally relate to the world around them. It's not human nature to delve into 47-point economic reform plans, attractive as they are to highly educated policy wonks.

People tend to be visceral and self-interested. For example, consider what happened after Upton Sinclair wrote The Jungle, his 1906 novel about the horrors endured by Chicago slaughterhouse workers. Instead of helping workers, Congress passed the Pure Meat Act to ensure beef and pork were safe to eat. Said Sinclair: 'I aimed for the public's heart and by accident hit it in the stomach'.

Now think about Johnson cynically saying, 'there are no disasters, only opportunities. And, indeed, opportunities for fresh disasters', and Trump invoking the royal we at every rally to proclaim 'we love you'.

Shadows behind the populists

Behind their rise is a corporatised world in which putting clowns and cowards in office – dupes who will do the bidding of those whose fortunes rely on the beneficence of government – maximises future profits. For more, read Adam Smith's The Theory of Moral Sentiments (1755), and An Inquiry into the Nature and Causes of the Wealth of Nations (1776). We need to be wary of campaign finance rules because people naturally respond, like dogs and parrots, to whoever feeds them. The practical but soulless entities we call corporations, and the people who control them, see morons like Johnson and Trump promoting their opportunities because in the long run government by clowns breeds cynicism about the prospect of strong and effective governments.

We should expect those already rich and those driven by a lust for power and money to behave as their nature dictates. But we shouldn't accept their greed and desire to advance clowns like Johnson and Trump. Instead, we should work on things as simple as making reading and writing common skills enjoyed by 17 or 18-year-olds, and on encouraging people to take pride in themselves as owners of our governments rather than renters or, God forbid, squatters.

About the Contributor

David Cay Johnston is the best-selling author of eight books, including three on Donald Trump. He is a Pulitzer Prize-winning investigative reporter, formerly with The New York Times, who since 2009 has taught at Syracuse University College of Law.

The magic of Boris?
It doesn't travel to NYC

**Johnson's 'charisma' was his calling card.
It charmed many journalists like
Angela Antetomaso, though the
charm has worn off for her**

I remember the day I tried to explain to my Italian husband, who I'd recently married and who had just moved to the United Kingdom, who Boris Johnson was. We were watching the evening news, and there he was, the London mayor: dangling mid-air on a zip-wire, wearing a dark suit, a harness and a hard hat, holding two Union Jack flags in his hands.

That was quite a scene. I found myself awkwardly blurting: 'They say he is incredibly clever. He seems a bit eccentric, but he went to Eton and Oxford, and he is apparently very intelligent'. 'Is he really?' my husband replied, flatly. His deadpan reaction surprised me, but I just shrugged and went on believing that Johnson was a top-notch guy: amusing, extremely bright and politically very skilled. How deluded I was.

Falling off his perch

Fast forward a few years and here I am, now living in the United States and having to explain again - this time to American people - who Boris Johnson is, what kind of Prime Minister he was, and why he suddenly 'resigned'. There are so many things to be said about him, but one thing I now know for sure, he is definitely not the smart, admirable man I once thought he was.

It needs to be said that, for the most part, Johnson's many indiscretions while in office didn't make it to this side of the Atlantic. At least not all of them. The petty little lies he churned out almost daily in order to keep himself afloat were too domestic to be exported, and too intricate to be fully explained to foreigners who are not familiar enough with British politics.

When in July 2022 the news of his abrupt downfall made it around the world, many Americans wondered what had really happened behind the scenes. Not that they had the greatest respect or admiration for him, anyway. In a country that is still dealing with the post-Trump era, and an electorate that is (for most at least) aghast at the idea of having Donald Trump running again for President in 2024, it is easy to see why.

'Britain Trump'?

The fact that back in 2019 Boris Johnson was hailed 'Britain Trump', by none other than Trump himself, didn't actually help. If the international media feasted on such a parallelism, US media embraced it. Likening Johnson to then-US-President Donald Trump wasn't that hard, after all. The blonde hair, the narcissistic behaviour, the twisted fabrications, the silly jokes, and the at-times-senseless mumbling were too easy a comparison to make.

Both were seen as erratic and temperamental, both were great masters at pompousness and self-glory, and both had an unscrupulous ambition. They generated numerous scandals, and made countless unpredictable slip-ups that many a time left the world open-mouthed. Looking a bit more in depth, though, that's not all there is to it.

If Trump was a billionaire, businessman, and entrepreneur-turned-politician who yearned to go down in history as the President who changed America, Boris Johnson was quite a different figure.

Born into a wealthy family, with a privileged and elitist upbringing, Johnson's life has always been entrenched in politics, thanks to his father's various jobs at some of the main European institutions.

His dream has always been to get to the top – to be 'World King', in his own words - and rumour has it that he would sell his soul to get there.

In a way, he did. While he initially believed that leaving the EU was a very bad idea for the UK, he changed his position mid-campaign as soon as he realised that the Brexit narrative could actually be his fast-lane ticket to Downing Street. In all truth, the main feeling is that he wanted to become Prime Minister just to add another notch on his belt, and most certainly not for his country's welfare.

A good PM?

He never seemed to care much about the role itself, he never strived to become a good, credible, and trustworthy leader. And at a time of unprecedented global emergency, he didn't appear very concerned with strenuously safeguarding his people throughout the entire pandemic. Not at all, actually. This is how it looked from this side of the Atlantic.

The virus is spreading countrywide? 'I am having a personal crisis, no time to attend emergency COBRA meetings'.

People are dying from the contagion? 'We need to keep the economy going, let's shake hands with Covid patients in hospital and let's go on with our lives'.

My government just announced a nationwide lockdown to stop the spread? 'Restrictions only apply to ordinary people, let's go party'.

And more recently, when kicked out of Downing Street? 'I am the absolute best you can get, and I won't go until a new leader is in place. Meanwhile I will lobby with my fellow Tories and pump up the 'Bring Boris Back' campaign'.

And so on.

Falling in and out of love with Boris?

In all of this, my simple question ultimately is: what is all the fuss about? As a foreign correspondent who spent most of her adult life in the UK, I have had the opportunity to see Johnson's rise to fame and power. I clearly recall his time as a journalist, and his swift and successful move into politics. Even so, I have to admit that I have never been able to fully grasp what all the fascination was about.

I could see how respected and admired he was. I could understand how the dry humour, the crazy hair, the goofy look, the posh stutter - usually paired with a smart quote, some quirky classical reference, and a bizarre demeanour – would make him intriguing, and captivating. I could definitely see that – and I did fall for it myself, in a way.

Deep down, though, I never really got 'why'. And I have the feeling that, like me, millions of other people around the world could never actually figure out what Boris Johnson's real charisma was.

When he won the UK General Election by a landslide in December 2019 I had just moved to New York. I remember that many people in America were quite astonished at the overwhelming approval he got.

After all, there they were, still trying to carefully handle what they considered a dysfunctional 'loose cannon' President. It was hard for most Americans to believe that the British people would be so keen to hand over the leadership of their country to someone so closely resembling their very own Donald Trump. Even so, the UK electorate's sweeping support for Johnson at that point was tangible, and proved that the magic was there, his charm still on. It didn't last long, though.

Media creation

Less than three years on, that bubble has burst – and in a quite spectacular way. Is that because, fundamentally, Boris Johnson was possibly only a media creation, and as such, was short-lived? Rather he was - and is - his own creation, and this has been the case at least since his Eton years. Even his pitiful ousting was eventually entirely his own making. The wild ambition, the self-obsessive vainglory and the half-truths that got him to the top, are the same that brought him down. In the end, the pathetic scene of his desperate attempt to cling to power stripped him of the little dignity he had left.

What now for Boris Johnson?

I doubt he will stop here and quietly disappear from the picture. But if Trump is frenetically working on his comeback, with his 2024 US Election campaign already in full swing, for Johnson the outlook is quite different. He will do everything possible to stay in politics, but the disappointment and the mistrust he leaves behind are wounds too deep to be healed quickly.

It is difficult to think he could still be rescued, and credibly make it again in politics. In Britain, a country where trust and truth are paramount, the three years of Johnson's tenure will be remembered as the time of the 'everything goes', the age of the 'government of the few', not the many, the era of the (too) many mishaps, blunders, and deceptions.

Never before in British politics have so many broken promises become the norm – and never before have such low levels of ethics and integrity been silently accepted and overlooked. Quite clearly, it couldn't last.

The British people, unlike their former PM, do have a moral compass, and it is not going to be easy for Boris Johnson and his chums to ever be trusted again. He might attempt a comeback – and he may also succeed for a while – but the risk that the country would then lose its hard-earned credibility is too high. Without a doubt, it is not worth that gamble.

About the contributor

Angela Antetomaso is an Italian journalist and television presenter. She lived and worked in London for 20 years before moving to New York City where she now works as a correspondent for Forbes. She previously worked for CNBC, Bloomberg, and CNN.

ACT SIX:
THE JOHNSON LEGACY

Brexit: Boris' malignant legacy

**When Paul Connew was asked by his oncologist
what he wanted to name his stoma bag he said,
'Boris, after someone I know who is determined
to become prime minister and could well achieve
it despite being totally unfit and full of shit.'
Having consistently predicted that Johnson's
dream was highly likely to end in a nightmare
of personal scandal and political chaos,
here he reflects on the end of that dream**

Boris Johnson cast himself as the roll up, roll up front of house showman for the official Brexit campaign group, a role that at least one relative privately confides had far more to do with his transition from the boy who wanted to be 'world king' to the clownish man-child prepared to settle for prime minister than any great passion for Brexit itself.

Johnson indeed fulfilled his ambition, taking Britain out of the EU on the back of a referendum victory that ranks as the biggest mis-selling operation in our history, winning a landslide general election on the all too predictably unfulfilled promise of 'Get Brexit Done', before achieving another historic feat by becoming the first prime minister to be fined for breaking the law in office.

Finally, Johnson managed another milestone by becoming the prime minister humiliatingly ousted from office by a mass revolt of his own MPs and ministers, not on the honourable grounds of policy differences but by virtue of a sordid and shameful litany of lies, sleaze, law-breaking, cronyism, incompetence, hypocrisy, and a gargantuan sense of self-entitlement.

Doomed from the start

Turning back the personal clock, my low opinion of Johnson began in

1990 when I was a young senior executive on the News of the World and Boris was a thrusting young Brussels correspondent for the Daily Telegraph. One of my reporters was investigating Boris's Old Eton and Oxford chum Darius Guppy over a suspected fraud and Guppy, subsequently jailed in New York over a fake $1.8m jewellery heist and fraud plot, had got wind of our investigation. Guppy turned to Boris to see if he could use his journalistic contacts to get a home address for our reporter, Stuart Collier, so he could arrange for a couple of heavies to beat him up and shut down the investigation.

The telling tale of the tape

In an infamous but character-informing taped conversation which became known as 'Guppygate' Johnson agreed to help. Far from being outraged, he expressed relief when Guppy told him Collier would only get 'a couple of black eyes and a cracked rib' and our future prime minister and disgraced star of the psychodrama known as 'Partygate' said, 'OK, Darry, I said I'll do it. I'll do it, don't worry.'

In the end the planned assault never happened, but when the tape emerged Boris sought to laugh it off, claiming he was only humouring his privileged crook of a chum. His then-editor Max Hastings took a dimmer view and disciplined him without sacking him. I wonder if he ever privately muses that if he had given his young Brussels staffer the order of the boot, the course of British history might have been changed for the better.

Stuart Collier anticipated an apology. But Boris doesn't do apologies. (Witness his embittered, graceless No 10 resignation speech that omitted the R-word).

The first slice of 'cakeism'

Over the years I've encountered Johnson at various political, charity, and social events. One Brexit encounter sticks in the memory. We were on opposite sides of a very early debate on the issue when a young woman audience member asked how the UK could afford to exit the single market and the customs union and achieve the sunny uplands future being heralded by Boris and his allies and his rival for the spiritual leadership of the movement, Nigel Farage.

The answer to that young woman's question exemplified the 'cakeism' bluster and boosterism we have since come to know so well and at great cost. 'The Europeans need us far more than we need them,' he reassured her. 'They'll give us the Brexit we want and we'll still get the benefits of the single market and the customs union as we go our own way too.'

He either knew it was palpable nonsense or a blatant lie. At its most charitable, this was a sign of Johnson's lazy disregard for detail grasp, leaving that to the likes of Dominic Cummings while, with the support of his cheerleaders on the Tory right and in the pro-Brexit Tory newspapers, Boris could indulge his flamboyant 'Jolly Joker' persona and pose ad nauseum in front of that battle bus with its bullshit '£350m a week for the NHS' slogan.

Heineken Man, the charismatic charlatan

Undoubtedly Boris and his 'Heineken Man' charisma was a big factor. For many traditional Labour supporters who voted leave, contempt for the austerity policies of Cameron and Osborne and the sinking feeling of being left behind, together with the immigration issue, were critical. But at least Boris looked an unusual celeb politico who'd be much more fun to go down to the Dog and Duck with for a pint and a few irreverent giggles.

It was a myth, of course, as more recent history has proven. But it was a masterclass in bogus personality marketing, since exposed by showing Boris to be the personification of elitism, privilege, cronyism, and self-entitlement. He just hid it brilliantly and millions of reasonable people swallowed it for so long, partly because they wanted to believe it and buried their emerging suspicion that Brexit the reality and Brexit the selling pitch fantasy were very different beasts.

From Brexit to Regrexit

The last dozen or so major opinion polls reveal support for Brexit and the Johnson government's handling of it is now consistently in the minority, some showing margins well into double digits. To a degree that reflects growing awareness of the messages of most economists and many business leaders and analysts that Brexit will increasingly cause far greater and sustained damage to the UK economy than Covid. Indeed, the Covid catastrophe did gift Boris Johnson and his government a spade with which to half-bury the truth about a Brexit that, for all the boasts, is about as far from done as a 60-second boiled egg. To an even greater degree, the current cost of living crisis is exponentially expanding the ranks of disillusioned Leavers via soaring bills, broken promises, hospital waiting lists, the indignity of the food bank trip, etc, while Johnson's Brexit is still the timebomb that could rip apart the UK.

In simple terms, the clear consensus among the majority of experts is that Brexit alone will mean UK economic growth could be stunted for up to 15 years, with a GDP performance at the bottom end of the world's 22 most advanced economies, a similar rating for overseas investment in Britain, higher inflation rates, and slower recovery prospects compared to the EU generally. Result? The average UK worker will be substantially poorer, quite apart from the negative impact of the Ukraine war and its unpredictable duration and economic fallout.

Boris gloats, Starmer stumbles

I winced as Johnson gloated over Sir Keir Starmer's misguided, outdated, and needless pronouncement that Labour would not only never seek to reverse Brexit but wouldn't consider either rejoining the Single Market or the Customs Union, despite all the expert evidence it would make eminent economic sense.

The Starmer statement was clearly aimed at reassuring remaining Red Wall still Brexit devotees. The timing, not long before the Johnson defenestration, was certainly unfortunate in the sense it reopened old wounds and rifts within Labour. And with the polls shifting against Brexit, even in disillusioned, Boris-betrayed Red Wall seats, why the hell bother?

It seemed curious, too, when influential Tory politicians, such as Tobias Ellwood MP and the arch former Brexiteer Tory MEP Lord Daniel Hannan, have floated the idea of exploring rejoining the Single Market and Customs Union without fully rejoining the EU. Predictably both were publicly savaged by Johnson loyalists and the Conservative Right inside parliament. Privately, however, some more thoughtful Tory MPs echo their thoughts.

A toxic 'triumph'

The emerging tale of the opinion polls suggests the public could be ahead of the political class in painfully recognising the World in 2022 as a brutally different place from the one in 2016, or even 2019, and the Hard Brexit of Boris Johnson is more toxic than triumphant.

If Starmer had played his cards better, he could have nicked that famously successful 'Labour Isn't Working' Tory election slogan designed by Saatchi and Saatchi for Margaret Thatcher in 1978/9. Only this revised version would read 'Brexit Isn't Working...well, not in the way THEY promised you it would', THEY being illustrated with mugshots of Johnson, Rees-Mogg, Patel, and the Cabinet.

As a senior Johnson loyalist turned defector put it to me: "Boris took particular delight in his 'Captain Hindsight' tag for Starmer and laboured it for all it was worth it. But if Starmer has any sense he'd U-turn on that speech and cast himself as Captain Foresight. Boris might feel he's being betrayed all over again, but this government can't afford to go into the next election pretending or campaigning on a Boris's Brexit record as a sacred legacy ticket."

Big Dog briefs

Maybe Boris fears that himself? Hence the 15 July post-downfall splash headline in the slavishly loyal Daily Express "BORIS MESSAGE TO NEXT PM: 'YOU MUST FINISH JOB ON BREXIT'" based, I'm told, on a personal briefing suggestion by 'Big Dog' himself. Close to tears, faithful Culture Secretary Nadine 'Mad Nad' Dorries rushed to lobby Lobby journalists with the idea Boris could yet return as a future prime minister (presumably after a Conservative election drubbing). It's a thought Boris himself might harbour. After all, his hero Churchill was the ultimate political Comeback Kid.

Constitutional carnage

Constitutional misbehaviour instigated and carried out by Boris Johnson was subject to much parliamentary and legal investigation and challenge. Steve Foster examines the role the media played in informing the public of possibly the greatest-ever attack on our unwritten constitution

Boris Johnson's tenure as Prime Minister witnessed unprecedented exposure of and challenges to the government's constitutional behaviour. These have included allegations of and investigations into 'Partygate', 'jobs for your mates', the uncovering of lies to Parliament over the 'Pincher affair', and the Prime Minister's inquiry into allegations of bullying by his Home Secretary, Priti Patel. Such incidents were often accompanied by judicial challenges, the courts responding by declaring much of this conduct in breach of the law.

Despite such challenges, the repetition of such behaviour has exposed the frailty of our constitutional democracy and the methods by which it is able to control abuse of power. Despite these flagrant breaches of constitutional propriety, Johnson remained in power until deposed by his own treacherous Tory party, exposing the weakness of our constitution. Yet have such events affected the public's perception of acceptable governmental and political behaviour, and will that be reflected in the result of the next general election?

Prorogation of Parliament, the Supreme Court, and public backlash

The issue of constitutionality and Johnson's tactics were raised most strikingly in the Brexit saga after the 2016 referendum. Once the government set its sight on a withdrawal plan, legal questions were raised as to whether that could be done without the approval of Parliament. In the end, both the decision to withdraw from the EU, by triggering Article

51 of the Treaty without Parliamentary involvement, and the decision of the Prime Minister to suspend Parliament in an attempt to frustrate Parliamentary debate on the government's withdrawal plans, were held unlawful. Both decisions caused great political and public debate, the courts being accused of undermining the democratic process. As an example of constitutional and political skulduggery, Johnson asked the Queen to prorogue Parliament early, having the desired effect of avoiding parliamentary debate as the deadline for triggering Article 51 would have passed by the time Parliament sat again. Neat trick if you can get away with it, but was this unlawful, or merely politically unconstitutional? The Supreme Court held that the Constitution was built on democratic accountability, including the power and duty of Parliament to control the executive. Therefore, Johnson was forced to act within the law. However, not being bound to resign for misusing his constitutional powers remained in charge and media reaction was, naturally, mixed.

Breaking court orders and acting without legal authority

During Johnson's reign, we have witnessed some extraordinary cases of government contempt for the rule of law. In April 2021, in what was described in the press as a 'landmark court ruling', it was found that the Home Secretary, Priti Patel, had frustrated a death in custody inquiry by attempting to deport a key witness to the investigation, ignoring a previous court ruling not to do so. This was not simply a case where the government had broken the law. Rather, it was an example of the government being prepared to set themselves above the legal process: ignoring rules in the belief that they cannot be accountable or sanctioned. The Guardian noted that this was the first time that a Home Secretary had breached a detainee's human rights by refusing to allow them to give evidence at an inquest, yet with what effect?

A further, extraordinary example of the government's attitude to the law was evident when Priti Patel, again, was accused of attempting to unlawfully evict thousands of migrants during the pandemic. Hearing cases challenging the lawfulness of the Home Secretary's policy, a witness statement admitted that at the relevant time 'we did not consider what power, or whether we had the power, to implement what we saw as administrative changes'. The judge noted that it was 'extremely troubling' if she was acknowledging that when she set up this system she did so without legal authority. This is not simply a case of being caught out after the courts have interpreted the appropriate legal power; rather it is a flagrant and deliberate disregard of the law. More recently, it was found that the Secretary of State had made decisions on climate change without being briefed upon crucial information about the contribution to reductions in greenhouse gas emission. Further, in reporting to Parliament, he failed to explain how his policies met emissions targets. These were clear breaches of the law, the rule of law and constitutional practice, and yet there was still no practical ramifications or punishment, and no real mainstream media coverage.

Breaking and then amending the constitutional code and jobs for your mates: the futility of judicial review

Johnson's role in the Priti Patel bullying allegation culminated in a judicial review of his decision not to use the Ministerial Code against her. Informed by the independent adviser on ministers' interests that she had breached the Code, even if unintentionally, the Prime Minister concluded that the Code had not been breached, and that she retained his confidence. Although his interpretation of the code was reviewable, the decision to dismiss or retain a minister in office was not, being a political matter for the Prime Minister. His conclusion that she had not breached the Code was not a finding that her conduct did not amount to bullying, but that it would not be right to record that the Code had been breached or that her conduct did not warrant a sanction such as dismissal. Thus the Prime Minister was the arbiter of the Code; and it was for him alone to determine whether a minister had departed from it to such an extent that he could no longer have confidence in her. This case is a further example of the existing government taking action in the belief that as we have spoken that will be the end of the matter, and the courts are powerless to intervene. The PM subsequently took the biscuit by amending the code to stop any future possibility of resigning for breaching its provisions: in future it will suffice to apologise.

Johnson's tactics in ensuring that his Tory mates benefited from the pandemic was also tested in the courts. Here it was held that the operation of a high priority lane – whereby suppliers of PPE referred by Ministers, MPs, and senior officials were afforded more favourable treatment for the supply of personal protective equipment – was in breach of the Public Contracts Regulations 2015. However, although the operation of the lane was declared unlawful, because it was highly likely that the outcome would not be substantially different (the contracts would have been awarded to them), the court refused to grant relief. The Court thus decided that the PM had acted properly, despite having acted under an unlawful policy that he in fact created!

The cases illustrate the limits to judicial review. In the bullying case, the Court cannot get to the truth of whether the PM was always going to support the Home Secretary whatever interpretation he gave to the Code. In the PPE case, the court does (or will) not consider the political allegations that allocation was made based on 'jobs for the PM's mates'. Those matters, presumably, as with the questions of what is a party, and whether you went to it, is left to political and public debate. No amount of media coverage and attack can get the job done, and Boris out.

Conclusions

Several tales of legal and constitutional challenge to Johnson and other Ministers acting under him have been considered. In terms of considerations about Johnson's character and antics it has been interesting to ponder the impact of these challenges on the public perception, and reaction to them via media coverage. In the absence of a legally entrenched constitution, and courts being incapable of invalidating unconstitutional behaviour, it is lack of public support, and, ultimately, through the ballot box, that governmental power is restricted. Yet for public and moral arguments to succeed, the media must play its role in exposing and highlighting constitutional impropriety. As Andrew Anthony wrote in January 2022, the media played a major role in exposing Johnson's lies over 'Partygate'. Others, predictably, defended the actions for political reasons. In any case, there is a limit to what media exposure can do to ensure accountability for constitutional misbehaviour.

Endnotes

(Miller) v Secretary of State for Exiting the European Union [2018] UKSC.
(Miller) v Secretary of State for Exiting the European Union [2019] UKSC
'Enemies of the People: fury over out of touch judges who have declared war on democracy' by defying 17.4m Brexit voters and who could trigger constitutional crisis' Daily Mail, 4 November 2016.
Diane Taylor 'Priti Patel's detention policies found to be unlawful', The Guardian, 14 April 2021.
R (on the application of Lawal) v Secretary of State for the Home Department (JR/626/2020(V)).
Jonathan Ames, 'Home Secretary broke law over death of detainee' The Times, 15 April 2021.
Diane Taylor, 'Judge criticises Priti Patel over policy for asylum seekers

in pandemic' The Guardian, 6 May 2021.
R (on the application of Friends of the Earth Ltd) v Secretary of State for the Business, Energy and Industrial Strategy [2022] EWHC 1841 (Admin).
ClientEarth, 'We've won our case against the UK Government's inadequate net zero strategy, 19 July 2022.
R (on the application of the FDA) v Prime Minister and Minister of the Civil Service [2021] EWHC 3279 (Admin).
R (Good Law Project) v Secretary of State for Health and Social Care [2022] EWHC 46 (TCC); R. (on the application of the FDA) v Prime Minister and Minister of the Civil Service [2021] EWHC 3279 (Admin).
Steve Foster, 'The Rule of Law in Modern Times: not a Priti Sight' (2021) 26(2) Coventry Law Journal.
Andrew Anthony, 'Scooped' it was the 'mainstream media' that brought Boris Johnson low', The Guardian, 22 January 2022.

References

Jonathan Ames (2021) 'Home Secretary broke law over death of detainee' The Times, 15 April.
Andrew Anthony (2022) 'Scooped: it was the 'mainstream media' that brought Boris Johnson low', The Guardian, 22 January.
ClientEarth (2022) 'We've won our case against the UK Government's inadequate net zero strategy, 19 July.
Editorial (2016) 'Enemies of the People: fury over out of touch judges who have declared war on democracy' by defying 17.4m Brexit voters and who could trigger constitutional crisis' Daily Mail, 4 Nov.
Steve Foster (2021) 'The Rule of Law in Modern Times: not a Priti Sight', 26(2) Coventry Law Journal.
Diane Taylor (2021) 'Priti Patel's detention policies found to be unlawful', The Guardian, 14 April.
Diane Taylor (2021) 'Judge criticises Priti Patel over policy for asylum seekers in pandemic' The Guardian, 6 May.

About the contributor

Dr Steve Foster is Associate Professor in Law at Coventry University, teaching Constitutional Law and Human Rights for over 45 years. He specialises in press freedom and celebrity privacy and the law, and the impact of the Human Rights Act 1998 and the European Convention on the protection of human rights in the UK. He is the author of Human Rights and Civil Liberties (Longman 2011), and has had his work published in several leading law journals.

Standards in public life – what on earth happened?

Boris Johnson's legacy is long-term damage to the concept and operation of ethical standards in government and public life, argues Alistair Jones

In 1994, in response to the many allegations of sleaze in his government, John Major established a Committee on Standards in Public Life, chaired by Lord Nolan. Nolan, in his first report, set out seven principles of public life. These are standards by which anyone in public life, from a school governor to the prime minister, can be judged: selflessness; integrity; objectivity; accountability; openness; honesty; and leadership.

Ministerial Code of Conduct

The Ministerial Code of Conduct (2019, 1) reinforces the importance of these principles for ministers and all members of government: 'The Ministerial Code should be read against the background of the overarching duty on Ministers to comply with the law and to protect the integrity of public life. They are expected to observe the Seven Principles of Public Life'.

There are also clear warnings to ministers in the Code:

It is of paramount importance that Ministers give accurate and truthful information to Parliament, correcting any inadvertent error at the earliest opportunity. Ministers who knowingly mislead Parliament will be expected to offer their resignation to the Prime Minister (ibid, 1)

Ministers only remain in office for so long as they retain the confidence of the Prime Minister. He is the ultimate judge of the standards of behaviour expected of a Minister and the appropriate consequences of a breach of those standards (ibid, 2-3)

Accountability for breaching the code

In all of this it is very clear as to the importance of both the Ministerial Code of Conduct and the Principles of Public Life. The convention of any breach is for a minister to tender their resignation, with the expectation the offer will be accepted. Yet the Johnson Government, probably more than any other government, has overseen more breaches of both Code and Principles and seen so very few resignations for such breaches (two: Conor Burns and Matt Hancock). Bearing in mind it is the Prime Minister who is the ultimate judge in the enforcement of these standards and who decides the punishment if there are breaches, the blame ultimately falls at the feet of Alexander Boris de Pfeffel Johnson.

One of the concerns, that has not always been picked up, is the Ministerial Code has been applied to some ministers but not to others. In May 2020, Conor Burns resigned as Minister of State for Trade Policy as he had used his position to intimidate a member of the public. This is very clear in the Ministerial Code (2019, 1): 'Harassing, bullying or other inappropriate or discriminating behaviour wherever it takes place is not consistent with the Ministerial Code and will not be tolerated'.

Failure to uphold the Ministerial Code

Yet when the then ethics adviser, Sir Alex Allan, found the Home Secretary, Priti Patel, to have repeatedly breached the Ministerial Code through bullying her staff, the Prime Minister disagreed with the findings. Allan specifically stated, 'her behaviour has been in breach of the Ministerial Code, even if unintentionally' (Allan, 2020, 1-2). Allan included a get-out clause by noting how Patel had not received any feedback about her behaviour and that her behaviour had subsequently improved. Yet the breach is still clear. Regardless of the possible lack of intent, it should have been a resignation matter as per the actions of Conor Burns, and the wording in the Ministerial Code. When the decision not to sack Patel was challenged in the courts, Johnson's defence was that he was not legally required to sack her. In relation to the wording in the Ministerial Code, that perspective is not wrong. It does, however, undermine the spirit behind the Code. There are clear standards of behaviour required of anyone in public office, and particularly serving in government.

There were further allegations of Patel breaching the Code by holding a meeting to discuss government business without any officials present. Patel's defence was that it was a private meeting with a donor to the Conservative Party and people who worked in the aviation industry

(Young, 2021). Again, the response from Johnson was to find her not guilty, and Cabinet colleagues were wheeled out in front of the media to defend both Patel and the decision taken by Johnson.

Prime Ministerial breaches of the Code

The Prime Minister was also accused of repeatedly breaching the Ministerial Code, through misleading the House (lying to Parliament), as well as being issued with a fixed penalty fine for attending a party of which he had previously claimed no prior knowledge.

Much was made in the media of the attending of this and other parties, but very little was made of the lying, and subsequent breaches of the Ministerial Code. In this respect, it could be argued the media collectively failed in holding the Prime Minister to account for his actions, as did all MPs. Focusing on the parties – 'Partygate' – was an easy target, but with so many parties and fines linked to 10 Downing Street, the lying and dissembling about the parties, and the related breaches of the Code of Conduct and the Ministerial Code, were seen as almost peripheral.

When Lord Geidt, former adviser to the Ministerial Code, raised the concern the Prime Minister may have breached the Code and should resign (BBC, 2022), the Prime Minister responded that it was not a resignation matter as 'there was no intent to breach the law' (Ferguson, 2022). This 'intent' defence gives an interesting interpretation of the law, and one that would probably never stand up in court. Ministers were also sent out on the airwaves to defend the Prime Minister. Their defence was to point out the Ministerial Code was there for guidance, the Prime Minister had apologised, and the whole event was unintentional and inadvertent. Thus, it was not a resigning matter.

One of the consequences of so many challenges to the Ministerial Code was for the Prime Minister to rewrite parts of it. The second version written by Johnson (Cabinet Office, 2022) contains references to the Standards in Public Life, as did its predecessor. The changes appear much more about defending how the Prime Minister may have previously breached the Code and outlining how that could not be the case. It also changes the penalties for any such breaches to include a more lenient set of alternatives.

Comeuppance for the PM

The fall of Johnson as Prime Minister was little more than a continuation of this approach to deflect and bluster when challenged on the Ministerial

Code and Standards in Public Life. The appointment and defence of Chris Pincher as Deputy Chief Whip appeared to have been the final straw for many Conservative MPs. Johnson subsequently apologised for making the appointment, adding 'I just want to make absolutely clear that there is no place in this government for anybody who is a predator or who abuses their position of power' (Morris, 2022). As with so many other occasions where the Standards in Public Life and the Ministerial Code had been breached, Johnson would offer an apology and assume that would suffice. This perspective is in the 2022 version of the Ministerial Code – 'available sanctions include requiring some form of public apology' (Cabinet Office, 2022, 3).

Sajid Javid, in his resignation speech, noted how Cabinet members had repeatedly given Johnson the benefit of the doubt over the lying and misrepresentation, but that it had eventually got too much for him. The problem is the damage done to standards of ethical behaviour cannot be undone easily, and all members of that cabinet are tarnished by such inaction. Yet anyone who knew the history of Johnson must have known the cavalier approach he took to rules. In a leaked letter from his Eton school days, one of the teachers observed how Johnson acted as if 'he should be free of the "network of obligation that binds everyone" ' (Gant, 2022). Yet the double-standards of both Johnson and his government went largely unchecked. The Johnson bluster and diversion appeared to be sufficient in parts of the media – and in Parliament – to enable him to continue to get away with behaviour that failed to meet the Standards in Public Life expected of a Prime Minister. While this approach eventually failed Johnson, it is the longer-term damage to Standards in Public Life that is of greater concern.

References

Alex Allan (2020) 'Findings of the Independent Adviser' available at assets.publishing.service.gov.uk/government/uploads/system/uploads/att achment_data/file/937010/Findings_of_the_Independent_Adviser.pdf
BBC (1 June 2022) 'Partygate: Boris Johnson urged to explain why fine did not breach ministerial code' available at www.bbc.co.uk/news/uk-politics-61653755_Cabinet Office (2019) Guidance: Ministerial Code
Cabinet Office (2022) Guidance: Ministerial Code
Emily Ferguson (2022) 'What is the ministerial code? Rules for ministers explained and what it means if Boris Johnson breached them' i-news.co.uk (1 June 2022) available at inews.co.uk/news/politics/ministerial-code-what-rules-ministers-explained-boris-johnson-breach-changes-1661733

James Gant (2022) " 'Boris seems affronted when criticised for what amounts to a gross failure of responsibility': Letter goes viral from PM's Eton classics master re-emerges despairing about his 17-year-old pupil's 'effortless superiority' " Daily Mail (13 January 2022) available at www.dailymail.co.uk/news/article-10398617/Letter-PMs-Eton-classics-master-emerges.html

Sophie Morris (2022) "Boris Johnson apologises for appointing Chris Pincher as deputy chief whip and said 'it was the wrong thing to do' " Sky News 5 July 2022 available at news.sky.com/story/boris-johnson-apologises-for-appointing-chris-pincher-as-deputy-chief-whip-and-said-it-was-the-wrong-thing-to-do-12646408

Gregor Young (2021) 'Boris Johnson defends Priti Patel in row over billionaire Tory donor meeting' The National 6 September 2021

About the contributor

Alistair Jones is Associate Professor in Politics and a University Teacher Fellow at De Montfort University in Leicester. He is a leading expert on Britain's relations with the EU and author of Britain and the European Union (2016), The Resurgence of Parish Council Powers in England (2020), and Contemporary British Politics and Government with Phil Cocker (2015).

Boris and the pit

The rise of Boris Johnson to the pinnacle of political power in the UK testifies to a very unhealthy relationship between the power of the right-wing press and the power of the political right. Mike Wayne argues that the fall of Boris Johnson hardly cures us of that problem but it is indicative of internal conflicts within this nexus of press and politics

Boris Johnson could only flourish at a time when politics has been turned into entertainment. In this he is comparable to Berlusconi in Italy, the media mogul who became Prime Minister three times (a warning perhaps that we may not have seen the back of Boris Johnson), and Donald Trump, who hosted fourteen seasons of The Apprentice before becoming US President.

Once upon a time it was still possible to believe that the job of the media was to scrutinise the actions of political representatives, create forums for debate and dialogue and give citizens the tools to make informed choices at the ballot box. This was called 'the public sphere' by communications philosophers and if it was always a bit of an ideal principle against which to critically measure the actual performance of the media, today the reality and the ideal is so far apart as to be a Grand Canyon style chasm.

No doubt our lax rules on media concentration and our weak to non-existent regulation of the private press which gave us the phone hacking scandal have done much to corrode the media's historic self-conception of itself as guardians of democracy. That is difficult to do when the media itself is a large-scale power complex interwoven with political power.

Dominic Cummings, the strategic brains behind Vote Leave in 2016 and Boris Johnson's key advisor before November 2020, famously told us that Johnson regards The Daily Telegraph (owned by the billionaire Barclay brothers since 2004) as his 'real boss'. It is well known that another former Prime Minister, Tony Blair, regarded The Sun and its owner (the billionaire Rupert Murdoch) in similar terms.

In this incestuous relationship between media and political power, the favoured communication tool is the 'photo opportunity' not the interview. The photo opportunity promotes the carefully manufactured image and bypasses the opportunity which journalists may still occasionally hanker after for a line of tough questioning. Someone once said that Johnson makes himself as large as possible in the media space before an election and as small as possible during an election.

Now you see him, now you don't

Before an election, Johnson is keen to engage in any photo opportunity that will project the desired image of him, typically a cultivated slightly comical figure that is supposed to indicate his distance from the slick professionalism of the on-message Westminster elite insiders.

During an election even journalists sense that elected representatives should do more than engage in photo opportunities and be willing to answer questions about their policies. This amounts to a degree of democratic scrutiny Johnson is always keen to avoid. While it is extremely easy to evade a question in the political ritual that is the House of Commons, a determined journalist can still prove irksome. So, it was no surprise that Johnson did everything he could to avoid potentially tricky interviews during the 2019 General Election. He hid in a large fridge at one point to avoid the 'Good Morning Britain' cameras who had Piers Morgan on the other end of them back in the studio. He also famously refused to be interviewed by Andrew Neil on the BBC during the same election.

Instead the photo ops rolled on, such as him driving a bulldozer through a polystyrene wall with the words Brexit on it. In the election and afterwards as Prime Minister, Johnson turned himself into the Mr Ben of British politics, dressing up in the costumes associated with various occupations and seemingly prepared to get involved in any job other than the one for which he was elected.

The face of an electoral coalition

Johnson's electoral success is explained not just by his image projection and scrutiny avoidance tactics, but also by his ability to be the face around which an electoral coalition could be assembled. Theresa May's face sunk the Tory fleet, Johnson's refloated it. Dominic Cummings said of Johnson 'we only got him in there because we had to solve a certain problem, not because he was the right person to be running the country'. Thanks Dom. What was the 'certain problem'? I don't think it was Brexit in the first instance; rather the problem was securing a solid popular basis for a right-wing agenda, the strategic aim for which Brexit was the tactical means. Austerity politics from the Con-Dem coalition of 2010 was eroding the likelihood that the Conservatives could secure a Parliamentary majority on their own. A vote on Britain's membership of the EU offered a seemingly cheap way to achieve that without redistributing wealth.

Following Cameron's Brexit referendum miscalculation, in 2017 Prime Minister Theresa May tried to use Brexit to secure a unique coalition between the traditional Tory constituencies in the South and traditional Labour constituencies in the North. Their loyalties towards the Labour party were snapping (as indeed they had already snapped in Scotland) thanks to years of New Labour neglect. But May was stymied by a number of factors.

One was her careless honesty in making it quite clear that her social care plan would hand homeowner assets over to the banking sector so that people could pay for their care in their old age. The alternative, raising taxes on the wealthy, had not of course occurred to her. The other problem was that the leader of the Labour party, Jeremy Corbyn, had not been in the job long enough for the media to have completed their demolition job on his character. Worse still, he went into that election promising to respect the outcome of the 2016 referendum and his team had the bad form to unveil a manifesto that offered a costed if modest redistribution of wealth from the rich to the rest.

May out, Johnson in

Losing the Tory majority bequeathed to her by David Cameron made inevitable the end of May and the ascension of Johnson to the highest political office in the land. The 2019 General Election was a replay of the same strategy, uniting the Southern Tory constituencies with the North. This time it was successful. In part this was because the media had had a further two years to smear Corbyn (absurdly and without evidence) as an anti-Semite. In part because Johnson, as we have seen, was a canny campaigner determined to avoid campaign scrutiny. In part also because Johnson had the right-wing press championing his cause (while Corbyn had no mass media backers) and perhaps above all, because Corbyn had been pressurised by his membership base, his Parliamentary Party and his Shadow Cabinet to offer a Second Vote on the question of the UK's relationship with the EU. That was the sound of those loyalties in the 'Red Wall' seats finally snapping.

So the Clown-Prince won an 80-seat majority, and a popular base for conservatism had been achieved, the like of which had not been seen since the days of Thatcher. Yet the basis of that popular vote was rather different from the majorities Thatcher secured. It brought into Parliament a different breed of Tory MP, it committed Johnson to a programme of 'levelling up', to raising taxes to fund the NHS and social care, and other measures that gave the Tory Party an identity crisis. These included extending tariffs on steel in an effort to keep 'Red Wall' seats on board, a policy reported with obvious distaste by The Sunday Telegraph shortly before Johnson was forced to resign. Perhaps Johnson should have listened harder to his 'real boss'? Internal tensions within the nexus of media and politics as well as personal rivalries (were Treasury officials linked to Sunak responsible for the Partygate photo leaks, or Dominic Cummings or both and/or others?) did for Johnson. But his personally morally dissolute character certainly accelerated the speed with which opponents could act. There would be no ten years at Downing Street for Boris and Carrie.

Schadenfreude

Johnson's fall does not redeem the media which has kept silent on the Tories' breathtaking attacks on the right to protest in the Police and Crime Bill and their 'keep mum' attitude to Johnson's serious security breach in 2018 when he met ex-KGB agent Alexander Lebedev at a party while he was foreign secretary. We may enjoy a taste of schadenfreude that Johnson's lies finally caught up with him, but politics and the media is still a deep dark pit we are falling headlong into.

References

Daisy Stephens "PM refers to Telegraph as his 'real boss' Dominic Cummings claims'" www.lbc.co.uk/news/boris-johnson-refers-telegraph-real-boss-dominic-cummings-claims
Edward Malnick 'PM imposes steel tariffs to win back Red Wall' The Sunday Telegraph, 26 June 2022.

About the contributor

Mike Wayne is Professor of Media and Film at Brunel University where he convenes the MA in Media and Public Relations. Recent publications include Considering Class: Theory, Culture and the Media in the 21st Century (2017), England's Discontents: Political Cultures and National Identities (2018), and Marxism Goes to the Movies (2019). His website is: www.mikewayne.info

Whiter than white?
An unintended legacy
of Boris Johnson's most diverse
Cabinet in UK political history

**Barnie Choudhury explains how politicians of colour
may have benefited from the Tory party, but questions
why they have done little for the communities
where they are considered role models**

S ummer 2022 presented the British public with the spectacle of a Conservative party leadership election where one of the final two candidates was a person of colour. Conservative party members had to choose between a rich, cosseted, and privileged south Asian who famously admitted in a documentary two decades ago that he never had working class friends, or yet another white woman who was once a Lib-Dem, once a Remainer, and someone whose epiphany saw her trying to pose as a latter-day Margaret Thatcher.

Why is race so important? Because it is part of Boris Johnson's legacy: he trumpeted his most diverse cabinet credentials from the rooftops at every opportunity. And race, sadly, continues to define the lens through which many, if not most, people of colour regard their status in their country, adopted or otherwise, and by which they are judged. Despite there being a minimum four generations of south Asian immigrants to the UK, wider British society still looks upon us as foreigners who will never be true Britons, the so-called 'ethnicity hierarchy'.

Johnson's legacy

What started with former prime minister (and Eton toff), David Cameron, ended with the most racially diverse cabinet in the history of UK politics. Indeed, at one time at least eight people of colour were appointed to the most prestigious political offices.

Neither Labour, the once obvious home of ethnic minorities, nor the Liberal-Democrats could claim this level of success or promotion of racial diversity. Such was Cameron's strategy of positive action (not positive discrimination, which is illegal), that of those eight, five entered the 2022 race for Tory leader. What that shows, without any doubt, is how far the Conservative parliamentary group has developed. Without doubt, this crop of MPs showed they were willing to get behind brown and black colleagues. Without doubt, it showed the slow, shifting change in racial attitudes. By promoting people of colour, Boris Johnson, as with Cameron before him, and Theresa May's decision to set up a racial disparity unit, demonstrated the Tory's determination to throw off the sobriquet of the 'racist party'.

The 'anyone but Sunak' brigade

During the leadership contest we saw the knives out for Rishi Sunak: Jacob Rees-Mogg and Nadine Dorries set up the 'anyone but Sunak camp'. There was speculation that the former chancellor 'lent' his votes to foreign secretary, Liz Truss, because he feared Conservative darling Penny Mordaunt. But perhaps the most bemusing thing was Channel 4 News' 'investigation' on Thursday 21 July. It revealed . . . big drum roll, please . . . absolutely nothing . . . except that you can have smoke but no fire. The report had two 'big reveals'. First, it got documents which showed Sunak invested in hedge funds. Yes, and? Well, it seems that Sunak paid all his taxes under American law. The classic line was slipped in: 'There's no suggestion that Mr Sunak did anything illegal'. Second, Sunak's parents, a mother who was a pharmacist and a father who was a doctor, paid for his education at Winchester. In a Twitter thread, presenter and investigations editor, Cathy Newman, tweeted a series of claims. Channel 4 News could reveal that, 'His supporters have claimed he gained a scholarship to top private school Winchester College, but Mr Sunak has confirmed to Channel 4 News he did not get one'. I hate to burst Newman's bubble but a simple search would have found that Sunak confirmed this 'revelation' on 3 January 2020 to Conservative Home. Investigative journalists want to be first but sometimes, as the former editor of BBC Radio 4's Today programme, Kevin Marsh, told The Society of Editors, we must know when to let go, rather than try to shoe, without success, a lame horse. Creating all that smoke means the broadcaster shaped a story that this brown boy cannot be trusted, that he is hiding something, that his closet is full of skeletons. If Sunak has one fault it is that he is guilty of having parents who wished the best for him. Mind you, Jacob Rees-Mogg worked cleverly, and from an early age, to earn his fortune. He too married into a fortune. He also went to a privileged private school. So, if a white guy can aspire, why can't we brown people, or is that not allowed? Further, why didn't anyone mention Liz Truss' affair with an MP while she was married and a Tory Councillor? Surely, unfaithfulness goes to the heart of trust?

Unintended consequences

Let's consider how the 'ethnicity hierarchy' affects people of colour in general, and this crop of minority Tories in particular. Caribbean and South Asians arrived en masse in the UK in the late 1950s and early 1960s. We were British citizens by virtue of being ruled by the former Empire. We came here expecting a warm welcome. We ended up facing racism. My personal experience is that I fought daily (yes, fighting using fists and feet) against those Britons who saw it as their duty to go P★★★ bashing.

Enoch Powell and others made sure that, despite labour shortages, subsequent immigrants needed visas and permission to come to Britain. Those who arrived were given menial jobs. The Labour party signed them up promising equality, and new arrivals fell for it. Trade unions made sure black and brown folk did the jobs considered beneath those of the white working class. Even today, Labour divisively takes the brown vote for granted, and it is pitting Asian against Asian. However, when it mattered, Britain did open its doors to those fleeing persecution, even if, in the case of Leicester, councils took out full-page adverts warning Ugandan Asians not to come. Yet south Asians in particular continue to stick loyally to Labour, for all the good it does us.

The Asian work ethic and 'whiter than white'

What south Asians learned is that their values of hard work, aspiration, and sense of family chimed more with the Conservatives than those clever enough to lie to them with empty promises. So, in the 1990s, we began to see that slow defection from red to blue. But our lessons were not complete. We needed to be 'whiter than white'. We needed to show that not only were we British, but we could also prove it beyond reasonable doubt.

What other explanation is there to the spectacle of a black woman equalities minister and one-time leadership challenger, Kemi Badenoch, denying institutional racism? What other reason could there be for the child of immigrants and first female south Asian Home Secretary, Priti Patel, playing to the rabid right in her party and country sending asylum seekers to Rwanda, a country which carried out genocide during a civil war? What other reason could there be than to have a business secretary, Eton mafia member Kwasi Kwarteng, bring in rules to weaken further trade union rights? What other reason could there be for the first south Asian Attorney General, Suella Braverman, saying she wants the UK out of the European Convention of Human Rights? Article 2, right to life; article 3, prohibition of torture; article 8, right to privacy and family life; article 10, freedom of expression: all in danger of being struck out. Horrifying. Yet these are hot-button issues which resonate with a Tory party still wishing for colonialism and Empire.

These people of colour learned how to survive and thrive in a country which is often openly hostile to those who are not white. They learned by watching Johnson, time and again, say whatever it took, to anyone who would buy what he was selling, so they could cling to power. These politicians of colour turned a blind eye to their leader's ability to lie, deny, and obfuscate continually, and in doing so took part in the conspiracy of showing immense disrespect to their bosses, the electorate. They colluded in a massive cover-up, telling us that we were fed up with Partygate. They surrounded and gave succour to a man whose only wish was to serve himself and not his country, excusing him by saying he made the right big calls. They see the ability to rewrite history, from the playbook of the American president, Donald Trump, as an electoral asset. We bought it hook, line, and sinker, until one brown boy had the guts to break ranks.

Honourable Javid

That is why Sajid Javid is an honourable man. Javid, the son of a Pakistani bus driver, never forgot his roots. Javid, like Nadhim Zahawi, never forgot he needed the minority press. When he became Health Secretary, Javid asked his team to set up a roundtable with journalists from the ethnic media. The decision to engage diverse publications happened when Zahawi was Vaccines Minister. At a Downing Street press conference he heard one of his colleagues gushing about Eastern Eye and Garavi Gujarat, our sister paper.

Javid wanted to learn why the government was failing to get its vaccination message across to black and Asian people. Over time his team returned to Eastern Eye asking whether we would cover other health disparities. An unintended consequence of Johnson's unwitting ability to create the most racially diverse cabinet in UK politics is the reason why some press teams understand the need to engage with minority journalists.

Embrace ethnicity

Senior south Asian Conservative parliamentarians have told me their biggest fear is that despite all that Cameron, and now Johnson, achieved, racism remains among grassroot ranks. From personal experience, racism is more subtle, more covert, and far cleverer than in the 1970s or even 20 years ago. Sadly, this new generation of politicians do not quite get that or do not want to see it, acknowledge it, never mind confront it. It is simply not the done thing to complain, old boy, is the refrain I hear from those south Asians using pseudo-posh-upper-class-accents.

They forget the lessons from the other side of the pond, where a black president wasted his chance to unite, heal and lead his nation. Had he embraced his race, rather than run away from it, who knows what might have happened on 25 May 2020 in Minneapolis. Similarly, unless politicians of colour here embrace their ethnicity and stop apologising for their skin colour, trying to airbrush it away, Cameron's and Johnson's efforts may all come to nothing. That is the biggest lesson these potential role models need to understand. Your skin colour is something to be celebrated, not abjured. That should be Johnson's legacy but will it be?

References

Blinder, S. Richards, L. (2020) UK Public Opinion toward Immigration: Overall Attitudes and Level of Concern. The Migration Observatory. Available at www.migrationobservatory.ox.ac.uk/resources/briefings/uk-public-opinion-toward-immigration-overall-attitudes-and-level-of-concern [Accessed 22 July 2022]

Jewers, C. (2022) 'Anyone but Rishi': Boris Johnson is 'urging defeated Tory candidates to back Sunak's rivals' and the whole No 10 team 'hates the former Chancellor for bringing down the PM'. Daily Mail. Available at www.dailymail.co.uk/news/article-11015807/Anyone-Rishi-Boris-Johnson-urging-defeated-Tory-candidates-Sunaks-rivals.html. [Accessed 22 July 2022]

Rishi Sunak: Inside the Tory leadership candidate's fortune (2022) [online] Channel 4 News. 21 July 2022. Available from www.channel4.com/news/rishi-sunak-inside-the-tory-leadership-candidates-fortune. [Accessed 22 July 2022]

Channel 4 News. (2022) Rishi Sunak: Inside the Tory leadership candidate's fortune. [twitter] 21 July. Available at twitter.com/Channel4News/status/1550197951666049024. [Accessed 22 July 2022]

Gimson, A. (2020) Profile: Rishi Sunak, rising star of the Johnson project. ConservativeHome.
Available at conservativehome.com/2020/01/03/profile-rishi-sunak-rising-star-of-the-johnson-project/. [Accessed 22 July 2022]

Marsh, K. (2004) Speech given to the Society of Editors – What makes a good journalist? BBC Press Office.
Available at www.bbc.co.uk/pressoffice/speeches/stories/marsh_editors.shtml. [Accessed 22 July 2022]

Ashcroft, M. (2019) How Jacob Rees-Mogg made his millions from trading shares as a schoolboy to ruthlessly walking out on the old family friend who gave him his big break. Daily Mail.
Available at www.dailymail.co.uk/news/article-7464339/LORD-ASHCROFT-Jacob-Rees-Mogg-millions.html. [Accessed 22 July 2022]

BBC News. (2009) Tory deselection meeting begins.
news.bbc.co.uk/1/hi/uk_politics/8361987.stm. [Accessed 25 July 2022]

Choudhury, B. (2022) Don't Pit Asian against Asian. Eastern Eye.
Available at www.easterneye.biz/exclusive-dont-pit-asian-against-asian [Accessed 22 July 2022]

@sundersays. (2022) Party representation. [twitter] 22 July 2022.
Available at twitter.com/sundersays/status/1550418422223306753. [Accessed 22 July 2022]

Hansard: House of Commons (2022) Commission on Race and Ethnic Disparities. [debate] 17 March 2022, 710, c1075. Available at hansard.parliament.uk/commons/2022-03-17/debates/A7C2D672-2A1F-41C5-908B-A42ED7585608/CommissionOnRaceAndEthnicDisparities. [Accessed 22 July 2022]

Browning, O. (2022) Suella Braverman says only solution to UK's immigration 'problem' is to withdraw from ECHR. Independent.
Available at www.independent.co.uk/tv/news/suella-braverman-tory-leadership-echr-b2123196.html. [Accessed 22 July 2022]

Choudhury, B. (2021) "Please get vaccinated," says Javid. Eastern Eye.
Available at www.easterneye.biz/exclusive-please-get-vaccinated-says-javid/ [Accessed 22 July 2022]

Choudhury, B. (2021) One is three Asians still not vaccinated. Eastern Eye.
Available at https://www.easterneye.biz/one-in-three-asians-still-not-vaccinated [Accessed 22 July 2022]

Choudhury, B. (2022) Is the UK ready for an Asian PM? Eastern Eye.
Available at https://www.easterneye.biz/exclusive-is-the-uk-ready-for-an-asian-pm [Accessed 22 July 2022]

About the contributor

Barnie Choudhury is editor-at-large for Eastern Eye, Britain's number one south Asian national newspaper. He was a BBC journalist for 24 years and won industry awards for his reporting of diverse communities. Barnie is a lecturer in journalism at the University of East Anglia, and an honorary professor of professional practice at the University of Buckingham.

Cold up north

Scotland has long been challenging terrain
for the Conservatives, but few Prime Ministers
have been as unsuited to navigating the
Scottish political landscape as Boris Johnson.
Stuart MacLennan considers Boris Johnson's
difficult relations with his Scots colleagues,
as well as the challenge posed by
Johnson to the Scottish press

Scotland fell out of love with the Conservative party long before Boris Johnson's political career even began. The Conservatives have not won an election at any level in Scotland since the 1950s. While the Conservatives spent 20 years with no more than a single seat in Scotland, there nevertheless remained a rump of traditional Toryism in rural Scotland and some leafier suburbs. It is somewhat unsurprising, therefore, that Theresa May, arguably the most traditional Tory leader since the Earl of Home, oversaw a modest revival in Conservative fortunes north of the border.

Boris Johnson, however, is most definitely unlike Theresa May. As a political leader, Boris Johnson is purpose built to tap into everything the Scots dislike about the English: footy-obsessed lager louts whose visible patriotism belies petty bigotry. We Scots also, it seems, lack a sense of irony). It is not surprising, therefore, that Boris Johnson's relationship with Scotland – with its unique media landscape – has been somewhat challenging.

With friends like these who needs enemies?

Boris Johnson began his premiership with only the most tenuous support among the Scottish Conservatives. The leader of the Scottish Conservative Party, Ruth Davidson, as well as the majority of Conservative Members of the Scottish Parliament, supported Johnson's leadership rival Jeremy Hunt. The schism between Boris Johnson and the mainstream of the Scottish Conservative Party became even more apparent when long-serving Scottish Secretary David Mundell was sacked from Johnson's first cabinet, and when Ruth Davidson resigned as Scottish Tory leader the following month.

Fractious relations with the Scottish Conservatives were to endure throughout Johnson's premiership. While the 2019 General Election resulted in a resounding victory for the Conservatives, in Scotland more than half of the gains made by Theresa May in 2017 were overturned. In May 2020, junior Scotland Office Minister Douglas Ross resigned in protest at the Dominic Cummings/Barnard Castle affair. In July, Davidson's successor as Scots Tory leader, Jackson Carlaw, was reportedly forced out of his role by Downing Street to be replaced by Ross. In September 2020, Advocate General for Scotland, Lord Keen of Elie, resigned over his discomfort with the Internal Market Bill. Notwithstanding the fact that the role comes with ministerial office and a seat in the House of Lords, Johnson struggled for a month to find a Scots lawyer willing to replace Keen.

In May 2021, the Scottish Conservatives pulled off a surprisingly successful Scottish Parliament election campaign, with the Tories comfortably retaining second place and clinging on to their 2016 seat tally of 31 MSPs. The Tories' success was most certainly despite Boris Johnson, however, with his fizzog conspicuously absent both from leaflets and the campaign. In January 2022, Scots Tory Leader Douglas Ross called for Johnson to quit over 'Partygate' but rescinded that call during the Ukraine war, before eventually 're-ratting' during the final putsch against Johnson in July 2022. Johnson was widely blamed for the Scottish Tories' collapse in the May 2022 Scottish local government elections, with one defeated Tory councillor publicly remarking '[t]hat bumbling oaf Johnson cost me my job' With friends like the Scottish Conservatives, who needs enemies? Well, either way, Boris Johnson had plenty of them in Scotland outside of his own party.

Appetite for destruction

Johnson's appetite for constitutional destruction was not limited to Brexit. Despite appointing himself the first ever 'Minister for the Union' upon his appointment as Prime Minister, throughout his premiership Johnson displayed callous disregard for the Union. Despite Scotland resoundingly voting against leaving the European Union, rather than seeking a compromise that might placate the difference of opinion strongly expressed north of the border, Johnson pursued a harder version of Brexit than his predecessor, driving support for independence to new highs

In September 2021, Johnson appointed Aberdeen-born Michael Gove Minister for Intergovernmental Relations, responsible for co-ordinating relations between the Territorial Offices like the Scotland Office and the UK's devolved administrations. Despite this, relations between the UK Government and the devolved administrations remained strained throughout Johnson's premiership. In addition to potentially breaching international law, the Internal Market Bill, over which Lord Keen resigned, was variously described as a 'power grab' by the UK government and an 'assault on devolution' Following the enactment of the United Kingdom Internal Market Act 2020, the UK government has begun directly funding projects in Scotland, Wales, and Northern Ireland that would previously have been administered by the devolved administrations. While bypassing the devolved administrations in this manner has attracted the wrath of the SNP ministers in Holyrood, it hasn't dissuaded SNP-run councils from applying for the cash

Challenging terrain

Scotland's media landscape is somewhat unique within the United Kingdom. On television, Scots are far more likely to get their news from STV than the English are from ITV, STV's Scottish news programme outperforming BBC One's Since 2019, BBC Scotland has operated a standalone channel, including its own news programme The Nine. Scotland's print media is also somewhat more diverse. At the quality end of the market, the UK papers are supplemented by The Herald and The Scotsman, as well as regional middle-market papers The Press and Journal and The Courier. At the tabloid end of the market, the dominance of The Daily Mail and The Sun seen in England is challenged in Scotland by the Daily Record.

While this somewhat different media landscape in Scotland has often proved difficult for UK politicians to navigate, Boris Johnson is, arguably, as much a challenge to the Scottish media as the Scottish media is to Boris Johnson. It is a truism that the press, in the words of Yes Minster's Sir Humphrey, 'pander to their readers' prejudices', but what is an editor to do when their readers' prejudices vary so wildly in different segments of the market? For years, this has been the quandary of editors of the Scottish editions of The Sun, in particular, whose Murdoch-imposed editorial line has long been to support the SNP – especially at Holyrood – while also backing the Conservatives in England. This balancing act is made all the more challenging thanks to Boris Johnson's uniquely staggering unpopularity in Scotland. The solution, of course, is to run an entirely different editorial line in Scotland to the rest of the UK, and merely hope that no one notices.

A dire legacy

There can be little denying that Boris Johnson has left the Conservatives in Scotland in a far worse state than he received it. Johnson's leadership led to the resignation of the Scots Tories' greatest electoral asset – Ruth Davidson – and left the credibility of her eventual successor in tatters. Johnson cost the Conservatives more than half of their MPs in Scotland, with the prospect of further losses at the next election looking increasingly likely. While since the 2014 independence referendum, the Tories successfully used the constitution to bludgeon the Labour party into third place in Scotland, Boris Johnson's leadership has resulted in the Tories dropping back into third, with Labour enjoying a somewhat modest but measurable revival. Crucially, having largely re-made the Conservative party in his own image, there is little to suggest the successor to Boris Johnson will be able to undo the damage done to the Tory brand in Scotland by Johnson's leadership.

References

Kieran Andrews (2020) 'Union Fears Forced Jackson Carlaw to Quit'. The Times [online] 31
June. available from www.thetimes.co.uk/article/union-fears-forced-jackson-carlaw-to-quit-r2js9qgbv [30 July 2022]
Neil Davidson, Minna Liinpaa, Maureen McBride, Satnam Virdee (eds) (2018) No Problem Here: Understanding Racism in Scotland, Edinburgh: Luath Press Limited.
Glasgow City Council (2022) Council Preparing Seven Glasgow Project Bids for UK Government's Levelling Up Fund [online] available from www.glasgow.gov.uk/index.aspx?articleid=29439 [30 July 2022]
Ipsos Mori (2020) Scottish Political Monitor [online] available from www.ipsos.com/sites/default/files/ct/news/documents/2020-10/scotland-spom-october-2020-tables.pdf [30 July 2022]
Simon Johnson (2019) 'Ruth Davidson and Most MSPs Back Jeremy Hunt amid Concern About Boris 'do or Die' Brexit Pledge'. Daily Telegraph, 27 June
Mark McLauchlin (2022) 'Defeat Blamed on 'Bumbling Oaf' Boris Johnson', The Times [online] 10 May. available from <www.thetimes.co.uk/article/defeat-blamed-on-bumbling-oaf-boris-johnson-mlsmjk5ll> [30 July 2022]
Mark McLauchlin (2020) Boris Johnson Faces 'Impossible Task' Finding Himself a New Law Chief [online] available from

www.thetimes.co.uk/article/boris-johnson-faces impossible-task-finding-himself-a-new-law-chief-5hznf26kd [30 July 2022]

Ofcom (2021) Media Nations: Scotland 2021 [online] available from www.ofcom.org.uk/__data/assets/pdf_file/0025/222892/scotland-report-2021.pdf [30 July 2022]

Scottish Government (2020) UK Internal Market Bill [online] available from www.gov.scot/news/uk-internal-market-bill/ [30 July 2022]

Michael Settle (2020) 'Johnson to Be Told to 'Stay Away from Scotland' in Run-up to 2021 Holyrood Poll'. The Herald [online] 5 November. available from www.heraldscotland.com/news/18850839.johnson-told-stay-away-scotland-run-up-2021-holyrood-poll/ [30 July 2022]

About the contributor

Dr Stuart MacLennan is Associate Professor of Law at Coventry University, and Secretary of Moray Constituency Labour Party. Stuart has been an election agent for the Labour Party over the course of several elections, and previously worked for the Labour Party in the Scottish Parliament. .

ACT SEVEN:
THE END IS NIGH

Four days in July

John Mair sets the scene for the final act of Boris Johnson as Prime Minister

In just four days in July 2022 Boris Johnson went from hero to zero. He was back in Blighty triumphant after triple summits worldwide then the Pincher affair bit him on his bum. Lying about his lack of knowledge about his Deputy Chief Whip 'Pincher by name, Pincher by nature' (Johnson's own words) blew up in his face. Lord Simon McDonald, the former permanent secretary to Johnson at the Foreign Office, nailed that untruth firmly with a letter to the PM and a BBC Today appearance on Tuesday 5 July.

Johnson was caught out and dead in the water.

His political death was initially slow then accelerated the next day as 59 ministers or quasi-ministers in his government - half the payroll vote - simply jumped ship and left Boris to sail the Titanic almost alone. Despite his acolytes in government and in the press urging him to stay and fight, survival was a task too much even for Quadruple Teflon Bojo. By the morning of Thursday July 7 the 'resigning' lectern at Downing street was being dusted off. By midday Boris was at it 'resigning' with some lack of style talking of 'when the herd moves it moves', in plain English meaning 'I've lost the support of my troops'.

How did Johnson go from the hero of an 80-seat majority in the General Election in December 2019 to unwanted Tory baggage in 2022? 'Events, dear boy events,' as Harold Macmillan once memorably put it. That, and losing the trust of the electorate.

Sir John Curtice is the doyen of the UK for reading the tea leaves and the polls. He has no equal. In his special essay for this volume he examines the number that show How Boris Johnson lost the electorate'. The opinion polls simply do not lie.

The steep decline started with the farrago over Owen Paterson in

November 2021. Boris whipped his troops to reject Paterson's suspension then took them down the hill again. The political and personal damage was immense. Here's Curtice on this: 'Although the decision not to suspend Mr Paterson was rapidly reversed, the damage was done. Approval of the Prime Minister's handling of his job dropped by ten points, while his party's lead in the polls disappeared. Here was a warning that bending the rules for a cause in which few believe was potentially politically costly'.

That disaster was closely followed by the December breaking of the flood gates of news on the Downing Street parties during the Covid lockdown. Lead by Pippa Crear of the Daily Mirror and Paul Brand of ITV News the revelations came tumbling out fast and how. Boris was well and truly dobbed by his own profession. Curtice again: 'Instead of being his party's unchallenged champion, Mr Johnson found himself in the eye of a political storm that threatened to make Conservative MPs nervous about their electoral prospects under his continued leadership'.

After several months of heavy political battering, a weak and ineffective Metropolitan Police Inquiry, and the senior civil servant Sue Gray investigating the sixteen lockdown parties which may have broken the Government's own laws, the PM continued to try to bluff his way through the morass he had created. Johnson attempted to shift the public narrative to 'draw the line' in his parlance on Partygate as Big Dog had got the other Big Calls right. The polls and the public were far from convinced. Curtice once more: "Despite repeated attempts thereafter to persuade voters of his case, Mr. Johnson was never able to dislodge voters from their initial judgement. Polls conducted in the early weeks of 2022, when the initial stream of allegations became a flood, repeatedly found that between three-quarters and four fifths believed that the COVID-19 rules had been broken and that between two-thirds and four-fifths believed that Mr. Johnson was not telling the truth - perceptions that were widely shared by those who had voted for him in 2019. Moreover, there now widespread calls for him to resign: across the 20 or so polls that addressed this issue in the first three months of 2022, on average as many as 62 per cent said that he should go, including 41 per cent of Conservative supporters".

Partygate was not going away however hard the Johnsonites tried to kick it into the long grass. Finally the Pincher affair – a senior whip being 'handsy' with young Tory male wannabes – put the nails into the coffin of PM Boris Johnson. Public credibility had been stretched to breaking point: 'What might otherwise might have been regarded as an unfortunate oversight had such a devastating consequence because it appeared to confirm the view that most voters had formed much earlier – that Boris Johnson was willing to bend the rules for no good reason and then could not be relied upon to tell the truth about what he had done. And whatever their past achievements, a politician who is neither respected nor believed is bound to discover that they have come to the end of their shelf life'.

And PM Boris Johnson discovered that in four straight days in July 2022.

Professor Ivor Gaber is a television journalist turned academic. A specialist in politics at both ITN and the BBC he was instrumental in achieving the televising of Parliament. He knows his political onions and he knows when politicians are telling the truth or simply porkies. He's developed the concept of 'strategic lying' for the likes of Bojo. Let him explain: 'My own working definition, for what it's worth, is that a 'lie', at least in terms of politics, is a statement about a matter of substance which the teller knows to be false and which is deliberately intended to mislead'.

How does this work in practice? Here's Gaber's Guide to Strategic Lying: (1) It must be about a matter of major public significance; (2) it must contain a sliver of truth; (3) it has to go viral; and (4) it has to be in line with its target group's worldview.

Boris Johnson is (or was) a master of the strategic lie and has been for much of his adult life from Eton to Oxford to Brussels to County Hall to the highest office in the land. Sadly for him, he got caught out in the end. Finally as the storm clouds gathered over Downing Street. Dr Carolyn Jackson Brown of Leeds Trinity University has been sampling face to face the views of the next generation of journalists: [W]hether they voted Conservative or not, Boris with his comedy hair, was perceived by our classes of 2020, 2021, and 2022 as a combination of lovable clown but with Churchillian overtones'.

The young students' perceptions (positive and negative) of Partygate only properly registered when the solo image of the Queen mourning her dead lifetime partner and husband The Duke of Edinburgh was juxtaposed with the image of the Downing Street party the night before. This was an immoral step too far in their view.

After Death through drowning in lies, what next for Boris Johnson? Let Paul Connew in the Finale take you through some possible scenarios to this very sad but comic opera: 'The one certainty now in the still unfolding Johnson story is uncertainty. As the No10 door closes behind him, enemies and allies alike are already shaping up to write the final chapter, a melodrama guaranteed; tragi-comedy too. Shakespeare himself would have loved to script it.'

The end is not nigh for Bojo. It is here.

How Boris Johnson
lost the electorate

Boris Johnson's governing style focused on outcomes rather than due process. Sir John Curtice describes how this helped maintain his popularity, until voters discovered he was wont to bend the rules for purposes in which they did not believe

B oris Johnson had come to seem electorally invincible. Not only did he win an 80-seat majority less than six months after becoming Prime Minister, but he appeared to be immune to the electoral blues that most governments suffer in mid-term. In the first two years of the parliamentary term that he secured in December 2019, the Conservatives were never consistently behind Labour in the polls. And although his party's lead had been on the wane since the previous Spring, when its popularity had been boosted by a favourable public reaction to its speedy rollout of a COVID-19 vaccine, at the end of October 2021 the Conservatives still enjoyed a four-point lead.

Yet, as Britain prepared to celebrate Christmas just seven weeks later, albeit in the teeth of another wave of the COVID-19 pandemic, support for the Conservatives had plummeted by seven points, leaving the party seven points behind Labour in the polls. Instead of being his party's unchallenged champion, Mr Johnson found himself in the eye of a political storm that threatened to make Conservative MPs nervous about their electoral prospects under his continued leadership.

Johnson's governing style

From the earliest days of Boris Johnson's premiership, it was clear that his focus was on outcome, not due process. His principal objective was to secure the delivery of Brexit in the teeth of a parliamentary stalemate that had already brought down his predecessor. In late August 2019, it was announced that parliament was to be prorogued, that is, not sit, for five weeks prior to a new session that would begin in mid-October. It appeared to the government's critics that such an unusually long prorogation was intended to avoid the threat of further parliamentary attempts to block Britain's withdrawal from the EU. In the event, the decision was overturned by the Supreme Court, but the episode did no discernible damage to the Conservatives' standing in the polls. For while, according to Opinium, 58 per cent of Remain voters were opposed to the decision to prorogue Parliament, 59 per cent of Leave supporters were in favour. For half the public at least (and the half to which Mr Johnson was trying to appeal), the end justified the means.

Much the same could be said of the oft-criticised procurement practices adopted by the government during the pandemic. Voters, naturally, wanted the threat posed by COVID-19 to be brought under control as soon as possible, and, as a result, were perhaps not overly mindful of how that was achieved. Certainly, the speed of the government's vaccine programme seemed to justify the risk that had been taken in buying a range of vaccines before it was known whether or not they would work.

The Owen Paterson affair

However, this style of governing that had hitherto served Mr Johnson well began to unravel in November 2021, when he persuaded his MPs to vote against the suspension of one of their colleagues, Owen Paterson, for a breach of the rules on paid lobbying. With the possible exception of working in the NHS, most voters are doubtful that MPs should have any outside paid work and are certainly unsympathetic to any bending of the rules on MPs' outside employment.

Even among those who had voted Conservative in 2019, 64 per cent told Opinium that Mr Paterson should, as proposed, be suspended from the Commons for 30 days, while 61 per cent advised JL Partners that Mr Johnson had been wrong to tell his MPs to vote against his suspension. Although the decision not to suspend Mr Paterson was rapidly reversed, the damage was done. Approval of the Prime Minister's handling of his job dropped by ten points, while his party's lead in the polls disappeared. Here was a warning that bending the rules for a cause in which few believe was potentially politically costly.

The threat of Partygate

Then, along came Partygate. Numerous claims that the COVID-19 lockdown rules had repeatedly been broken by those working in 10

Downing Street hit the media headlines when on 7 December ITV News played a video of a mock press conference in which the Prime Minister's spokesperson, Allegra Stratton, referred to – and giggled nervously about – a pre-Christmas gathering that had been held the previous year when tight public health measures were still in place. Meanwhile, the following day, Mr Johnson assured the House of Commons in reference to one allegation that 'whatever happened, the guidance was followed and the rules were followed at all times'.

These allegations of breaches of the COVID-19 rules were potentially toxic. Just as there was no body of voters who were sympathetic to MPs' second jobs, there were few who were likely to feel that there was no need for those working in 10 Downing Street to adhere to lockdown regulations that everyone else had been required to follow. Moreover, it was an issue with emotional resonance, as voters (and some MPs) reminded the Prime Minister of the painful sacrifices that they had made not visiting parents in their care home, not comforting a dying partner in hospital, and not attending a close relative's funeral. Voters were unlikely to be forgiving if they were to believe that while they followed the rules at considerable personal cost, those working in Downing Street had sometimes been partying well into the night.

Voters' disbelief

Unfortunately for Mr Johnson, most voters came to the conclusion at the outset that the rules had been broken. Within days of the publication of the initial revelations in early December, YouGov reported that 75 per cent believed that a party that broke the rules probably had been held the previous year, a view shared by as many as 61 per cent of those who had voted for Mr. Johnson's Conservative party in 2019. Ipsos reported similar figures of 70 per cent and 62 per cent respectively. Meanwhile, Survation found that 78 per cent believed there had been a party while 75 per cent reckoned that the rules had been broken. These findings were echoed by other polls.

Meanwhile, perhaps even more seriously for Mr. Johnson, the issue was not only raising once again the issue of his apparent willingness to flout rules and regulations, but was now also threatening to damage his credibility. No less than 68 per cent told YouGov he was not telling the truth, including nearly half (46 per cent) of Conservative supporters. At 63 per cent and 46 per cent respectively, the equivalent figures from Opinium were not dissimilar. The suggestion from Mr. Johnson that any 'gatherings' that may have been held constituted a 'work event' rather than a 'party' became the butt of many a widely-shared joke.

Moreover, voters were already beginning to suggest that the allegations might be a resigning issue. Opinium found that 58 per cent believed that anyone who attended a Downing St party that broke the rules should resign, a figure that included 45 per cent of those who had voted in 2019. Even when Focaldata asked whether Boris Johnson himself should resign if parties had been held in Downing Street, well over half (58 per cent) said that he should, including nearly two in five (38 per cent) 2019 Conservative voters.

Suffering electoral damage

Despite repeated attempts thereafter to persuade voters of his case, Mr. Johnson was never able to dislodge voters from their initial judgement. Polls conducted in the early weeks of 2022, when the initial stream of allegations became a flood, repeatedly found that between three-quarters and four fifths believed that the COVID-19 rules had been broken and that between two-thirds and four-fifths believed that Mr. Johnson was not telling the truth - perceptions that were widely shared by those who had voted for him in 2019. Moreover, there now widespread calls for him to resign: across the 20 or so polls that addressed this issue in the first three months of 2022, on average as many as 62 per cent said that he should go, including 41 per cent of Conservative supporters.

This adverse mood was reflected in both Mr. Johnson's personal popularity and that of the Conservatives. In the immediate wake of the worst of the media storm in January 2022, just 23 per cent of all voters told Opinium that they approved of how Mr. Johnson was handling his job, while 61 per cent disapproved. Even more remarkably, at one point that month just 32 per cent of 2019 Conservative voters said they approved of Mr. Johnson's performance, while 52 per cent disapproved. Although for the latter group at least much of that damage was soon reversed – helped perhaps by the Prime Minister's role in the Ukraine crisis following the Russian invasion in February – his approval rating never returned to what it had been before the Owen Paterson affair.

Meanwhile, the Conservatives found themselves persistently behind in the polls. At one point in mid-January the party's standing slipped to as low as 31 per cent, leaving it as much as ten points behind Labour. And although here too there was improvement in the immediate wake of the Ukraine crisis, by the end of June, shortly before Mr. Johnson's downfall, the party was back down to 33 per cent and trailing Labour by six points. Mr. Johnson's electoral magic had seemingly deserted him.

Mr Johnson's fall

Of course, ultimately it was not the electorate's verdict that brought Mr. Johnson down, although two by-election defeats at the end of June helped drive home to MPs the message of the polls. Rather it was the discovery that Mr. Johnson had not only been less than honest about his knowledge of past allegations of sexual impropriety against the man he had appointed as Deputy Chief Whip, Chris Pincher, a discovery that precipitated a mass exodus of ministers. But what might otherwise might have been regarded as an unfortunate oversight had such a devastating consequence because it appeared to confirm the view that most voters had formed much earlier – that Boris Johnson was willing to bend the rules for no good reason and then could not be relied upon to tell the truth about what he had done. And whatever their past achievements, a politician who is neither respected nor believed is bound to discover that they have come to the end of their shelf life.

About the contributor

Sir John Curtice is Professor of Politics at the University of Strathclyde, and Senior Research Fellow at NatCen Social Research and 'The UK in a Changing Europe'. President of the British Polling Council and co-editor of the annual British Social Attitudes report series, he is a regular media commentator and academic author on polls and public opinion in Britain. He is also Chief Commentator at the whatukthinks.org/eu and the what scotland thinks.org websites.

Dead cats, red buses,
and strategic lying

**Some commentators ascribe Johnson's marginal
relationship with the truth to habits of dissembling
acquired in his schooldays and never forgotten.
Not so, argues Ivor Gaber, who here presents
the case for Johnson's use of something
far more deliberate – the strategic lie**

We all know the old adage of 'Lies, damned lies, and statistics'. We now need a new version: 'Lies, damned lies, and Boris Johnson'. Our former Prime Minister took bullshit, dissembling, exaggeration, and lies to new heights so frequently that any listing of them would be superfluous. But not all Johnson's lies were 'off the top of the head lies' as some have suggested. Johnson, or at least those advising him, developed a more sophisticated version of telling untruths which a colleague and I have dubbed 'strategic lying' (Gaber and Fisher 2021).

Dead cats first

Strategic lying is a sophisticated, and far more lethal variant of the notorious 'dead cat strategy' developed by Johnson's spin meister, Lynton Crosby, designed to distract the attention of both the media and the public when a politician or a party is under pressure. Johnson himself blew the gaffe on the strategy in the Daily Telegraph (13 March 2013) whilst he was still playing at being Mayor of London:

> There is one thing that is absolutely certain about throwing a dead cat on the dining room table – and I don't mean that people will be outraged, alarmed, disgusted. That is true, but irrelevant. The key point, says my Australian friend [Lynton Crosby], is that everyone will shout, 'Jeez, mate, there's a dead cat on the table!' In other words, they will be talking about the dead cat – the thing you want them to talk about – and they will not be talking about the issue that has been causing you so much grief.

But strategic lying is more, far more

I suspect but cannot prove that the strategy was designed by Johnson's subsequent eminence grise Dominic Cummings, who might not have formulated the strategy in the terms that I have set out, but knew what he was doing, and did it with devastating effect.

That £350m bus

Perhaps the classic strategic lie, or the one that I first noticed, was the infamous red bus that was the pride and joy of the Leave campaign during the Brexit referendum. It was emblazoned with the slogan: 'We send the EU £350 million a week. Let's fund our NHS instead'. Was it a lie or was it propaganda? There have been mountains of articles and books published on the subject of what constitutes a lie, with no definitive distinction being agreed. My own working definition, for what it's worth, is that a 'lie', at least in terms of politics, is a statement about a matter of substance which the teller knows to be false and which is deliberately intended to mislead.

There was some dispute as to the truthfulness of the £350 million claim. Leave campaigners argued, correctly, that our weekly bill to the EU was indeed £350 million or thereabouts. But Remainers cited that fact that the £350 million was merely notional because it didn't take into account all the rebates, subsidies etc., that came back to Britain. Thus the 'real' bill was closer to half the Brexiteers' figure.

No matter, for the purpose of the slogan was not just simple propaganda but was what I am calling a strategic lie, the key function of which is to grab the news agenda, not just momentarily à la dead cat, but for a sustained period and, just as importantly, to force your opponent onto your territory to counter the lie. As a tactic it worked brilliantly.

At the opening of the Leave campaign ITN's Tom Bradby interviewed Boris Johnson sitting on that bus and, over an eight-minute period, succeeded in demolishing his arguments about the validity of the £350 million figure. Leave campaigners might have been deflated but they shouldn't have been, for they had succeeded in making the cost of Britain's membership one of the main planks of their campaign and that was where it remained.

Indeed, Remain campaigners can be seen, in retrospect, to have fallen into the Leave trap by making the economic cost and benefits of Britain's membership the central issue of their referendum campaign. A day after the vote (24 June 2016) BBC News ran an online article: 'Eight reasons

Leave won the UK's referendum on the EU'. Reason one was that Remain lost the economic debate, and reason two was '£350m NHS claim gets traction'.

Not just the bus

And the £350 million figure was not the only strategic lie during the Brexit campaign. There were Leave campaign posters saying: 'Turkey (population 76 million) is joining the EU'. Apart from the fact that the population of Turkey is 86 million, the slogan is an overall outright lie in that 'is joining' is incorrect; 'would like to join' might be closer to the truth but still some way. Accession to the EU is a very lengthy process so if Turkey were to join it would be many years hence, and anyway, Turkey is showing a distinct lack of enthusiasm for the project. Finally, and most definitively, several countries, including France and the UK, have said they would veto any such move. But all this is irrelevant to the fact that it was a very successful strategic lie as well as a racist dog whistle, i.e. people got the implication without the need for it to be spelled out in any detail.

Strategic lies could also be identified during the 2019 UK General Election campaign. Perhaps the most well-known one was the Tory pledge to build 40 'new hospitals'. It was indeed true that there were either plans, or requests from hospital trusts that were being considered, which could amount to forty (although that included schemes entailing re-building existing hospitals). But once all these caveats were removed the true total of new hospitals being built was six – and that remains the number almost three years later.

Strategic lying defined

But back to the notion of the strategic lie.

For a lie to be so classified it requires four characteristics. First, it must relate to a matter of major public significance. A strategic lie has to be about a subject that is central to the political debate, otherwise it will just wither and die. Second, as is the case with the £350 million claim, it must contain a sliver of truth. If it doesn't it will just be dismissed out of hand. Third, it has to go viral, to be repeated and amplified by supporters and, paradoxically, also amplified by opponents who, in seeking to rebut the lie, simply reinforce it. Finally, it has to be in line with how its target group views the world. In this case, those who were likely to be in favour of Britain's withdrawal, would not have been surprised to hear that we were spending what appeared to be such large sums on our EU membership.

The 'secret' of the strategic lie

Since the recent prominence of 'fake news' (which is in fact not a new phenomenon) social psychologists have turned their attention to why people believe such 'news' and their findings can help us understand why the strategic lie is so effective.

To begin with, once a lie has been established in the minds of those potentially sympathetic to its message it is very difficult to get them to change their minds. 'That seems to make sense' the recipient is likely to say to themselves. Consequently it doesn't take long for them to 'take ownership' of the lie as the jargon has it.

Then, as mentioned above, rebuttal can be a two-edged sword. Certainly it provides an opportunity for the false claims to be challenged and corrected, but its more important effect is to reinforce the lie in the minds of the 'true believers'. To do otherwise is to invite the believer to experience the discomfort of cognitive dissonance, something we all seek to avoid.

Furthermore, no matter how authoritative and impactful the rebuttal might be, just by referring to it means that it maintains its place in the news agenda, to the exclusion of issues that the opponents would prefer to see discussed.

Lastly, if the media supports the claim that the lie is in fact a lie this simply reinforces the notion for supporters of the lie that the media is biased against them, their views, and their favourite politician.

What is to be done?

Strategic lying places conscientious journalists and regulators - both of the media and of elections – in something of a dilemma. What should they do?

Should they report the lie in the interests of 'fair' political coverage? This is what the BBC did during the EU referendum and this led them to being accused of peddling 'phoney balance'. Phoney balance might look like impartiality in action but balancing truth with lies is to give lies the same status as the truth which is just plain misleading.

Or should they call out the politician as a 'liar'? During an election campaign this could simply result in a referral to both Ofcom, the media regulator, and the Electoral Commission, for failing to meet the impartiality requirements for elections and referenda campaigns.

Or should they report the lie as such but add in fact-checking material? This again could run foul of the regulators and would no doubt result in the fact-checkers simply being branded as part of the biased media.

Or should they balance the lie with a rebuttal from an opponent? But this again runs the same risks and would make election news bulletins wordy and worthy and highly unwatchable.

Or, finally, should they refuse to report the lie and just ignore the lying politician? Again this might run foul of the regulators and, in addition, if the liar is a politician vying for the top job then simply ignoring what she or he is saying arguably does a disservice to the audience and to the democratic process.

The only answer is not writing new laws, but effective media and electoral regulation, written for the new times we are living through. It also requires a recognition that there is no 'objective truth' out there, only statements that are factually correct and that do not seek to mislead the audience one way or another.

But for now we are left with this graphic description of recent election campaigns penned by the late Dawn Foster in Jacobin magazine:

> [S]lash and burn and lie with impunity. Tell whatever falsehood you fancy, especially one that has a propensity to go viral. Get your smear heard as widely as possible, and if you're challenged, just lie. Far more people will see your initial lie than the follow-up correction, and few people will take the time to research any statistical embroidery or rewriting of the party's stance or record.

References

Ivor Gaber and Caroline Fisher (2021) ''Strategic Lying': The Case of Brexit and the 2019 U.K. Election', International Journal of Press/Politics, published online 17 March 2021.

About the contributor

Ivor Gaber is Professor of Political Journalism at the University of Sussex. He has been covering elections for the BBC and ITN since 1983.

'Whose lie
is it anyway?'

Boris Johnson came to power on a slogan (Get Brexit Done), and left under the shadow of several more. But who wrote them and did they have any sway? This joint research by UK university students doing journalism degrees at Leeds Trinity University explores different ways media outlets have characterised who 'Boris' is and what he has done, particularly through their headlines. Their module leader Carolyn Jackson Brown takes up the story

The way Boris has been portrayed in the media is of course, partly of his own making. But however performative his own actions, what will be shown here is that objectivity within journalism is apparently nowhere to be seen. Decisions about images and where to place them, adjacent or apart from either careless or contrived copy, all affect what we think of as true. Over several recent years we have found that BoJo's antics, in particular, have given journalists plenty of clickbait headlines, with the small print underneath very often not matching particularly well.

'Get Brexit Done' was the first line that some of our undergraduates had heard in relation to their incoming Prime Minister. Perhaps, because he was an ex-journalist himself, Boris realised the value of the clickbait headline to such a degree that he allowed himself to be persuaded to dispense with policy to adopt just this one line. However, it was not long before his persona became attached to many others, with some, including 'Partygate', potentially contributing to his eventual downfall. These lexical shortcuts fix meanings and assumptions and provide perfect fodder for student analysis, a skill of critical value, I believe, to the trainee journalists who will be the next generation to craft such lines.

So let's start with Brexit

Opening a copy of The Daily Mail in front of a class of journalism students had not provoked much of a response within my class of 2016 until they noticed a large photo of immigrants packed onto a dinghy surrounded by copy relating to the upcoming Brexit referendum. At first glance, conflating these two stories would not, they conjectured, matter too much since only people like their parents read this type of tabloid literature anyway. However, they went on to realise how journalists can and do affect democratic processes, via insinuated meanings through their use of headlines, images and text: not just to shape voters' opinions but also creating public discourses that then twist and turn and echo across a range of online digital spaces.

Our 'Journalism in Context' students examine broadsheets and tabloids online every year, deconstructing the juxtapositions of headlines, pictures, and 'facts', looking for evidence of bias, hidden emphasis, and other constructed meanings. They also consider whether some of these messages may affect political outcomes, or at least the timing of them. Boris Johnson, initially characterised as the 'bumbling buffoon', has provided more than enough material, and we also asked how much of the downfall of any Prime Minister might come from the momentum built up through disgruntled repetitions in the press and online.

Whose lie is it anyway?

By the time we got to 2019, we were in 'Boris lied to the Queen' territory, where our Leeds Trinity lexical analysts, from their readings across a range of news sources, could not agree on what it was he had lied about, if, in fact, he had done so at all (on that occasion). A politically motivated prorogation had been triggered, the length of which was later deemed to be unlawful. This much was certain, but what was the lie? The front page of The Daily Mirror with the above infamous headline, drills down with 'Court ruled PM misled monarch over motives' (12 September 2019). However, in direct contradiction, The Guardian later quotes verbatim the justices ruling that 'we are not concerned with the prime minister's motive in doing what he did' (24 September, 2019), and that these motives were not being assessed. This latter article also suggests that it was the Privy Council's decision to ask the Queen to suspend parliament, and not the PM's in fact. So, who is lying to whom and about what? Branding people as angels or devils is an all too familiar affair, but in this case who was the victim and who were the villains?

Sometimes blame is attributed not by alleged behaviour but by character inference. Whether they voted Conservative or not, Boris with his comedy hair, was perceived by our classes of 2020, 2021, and 2022 as a combination of lovable clown but with Churchillian overtones. As such there was a mixture of approval and fault-finding amongst the students. But were broadsheet and tabloid reporters impartial in their assessments and did they suggest approval or blame?

It is common knowledge that photographs can never be neutral, so it was particularly well observed that similar images of Boris, with his head in his hands, were used to portray both positive and negative spins, in one case, on the same story.

To coin a phrase: Another fine mess

We looked back and found, on 25 September 2019, The Times had labelled a head in the hands shot with 'PM flies back to chaos'. Here the problems are outside the politician, rather than within him as his fault, and he was potentially going to be The Saviour. The Metro by contrast borrows the old Laurel and Hardy trope from their 1930 film Another Fine Mess. Johnson's messy hair, that he is wrestling with, implied to all our students, even those unfamiliar with the film reference, that this time the mess was the Prime Minister's. For those who caught the cultural accusation, there is also the blame, on the head scratching culprit, for having 'gotten us into' this mess. The Metro piece goes on to pass on 'calls to resign', which seems common sense amongst these juxtapositions. Across other publications, some said Boris was dealing with the chaos, others that he was the chaos.

Perhaps these subtle positionings of blame and guilt are sometimes overanalysed when one considers the speed at which breaking news needs to be uploaded online. However, throughout our module we found careless reporting as well as careful concoctions of both truth and omission. It was also noted that the habit of providing hashtag labels from 'Brexit' to 'Partygate' or coining longer phrases such as 'The Cost of Living Crisis', and reusing them endlessly, shapes the news agenda and discourse in an increasingly reductive way. The reign of Boris was wrapped up in this equivalent of fish 'n' chips newsprint, and other news items often omitted altogether.

Partygate or Funeralgate?

The journalists of tomorrow probably won't know about President Nixon and the Watergate Affair, unless it reappears on Netflix as a boxed set. But they may lock a story into the news agenda and keep it trending on Twitter, if they can come up with a word ending in 'gate' that recalls it. We asked, would Partygate have kept its momentum if it hadn't had a name to keep it on the front pages and in the global running orders.

A particularly distinctive aspect, that we noted on 14 January 2022, was the implied treason in the image attached to the following words in The Telegraph 'Downing Street staff drank alcohol into the early hours at two leaving events'. There was not a photograph of the staff, the party, or of drinking culture, as the students might have expected, but instead a starkly empty St. George's Chapel, with the Queen, in black, sitting alone at one end of a lonely looking pew. The Prime Minister had not only betrayed the country in general here, but in particular The Queen, again, as when he had 'lied' to her three years earlier. National identity and our British Constitution were at stake, but then these were allegiances that Boris had attached to himself and his role, and journalists used them against him.

It was obvious that Boris played the media, with his chaotic hair and his Classical quotations, but we were seeking to establish how journalists played with him too. In their essays our students will inevitably discuss any observations they make about representations of people in the media along the lines of whether views and values held by society are reflected or constructed within the published narratives. But the clickbait headlines had a life of their own, making demands on what we should think about next, especially when it came to Boris. Maybe some of them helped precipitate the change in leadership this time.

About the contributor

Dr Carolyn Jackson Brown is Senior Lecturer in Journalism at Leeds Trinity University and author of Disability, The Media & The Paralympic Games, which focuses on Channel 4. Following a career in factual broadcast television, starting at the BBC, she now researches representation and diversity in the media and teaches critical analysis in journalism, media, and sport.

FINALE

Whither the (failed) world king?

What next for the Icarus of British politics? With his wings burned by the sun of truth, will Boris Johnson retreat into the sunset or will he be a huge shadow over his successor? Paul Connew reads the runes and asks, 'Whither Boris?'

Hasta la vista, baby. Those words, quoting Arnold Schwarzenegger's Terminator 2: Judgment Day character, with which Boris Johnson closed his final Prime Minister's Questions on 20 July 2022 intrigues, inspires, or terrifies, according to the audience. A typically Johnsonian joke or a threat/promise/delusion from someone whose colossal ego and sense of entitlement makes him determined not to be terminated but to rise Arnie-like from apparent destruction?

The joke notion is the one favoured by those in the Conservative party and beyond who earnestly desire that Boris Johnson disappear from the public stage after his self-inflicted defenestration, triggered by his debasement of the office of Prime Minister, his lies, abuse of power, and contempt for the normal rules.

But the former Tory leader and Foreign Secretary William Hague, who predicts Johnson will become a 'permanent nightmare' for the government, says Boris 'lives his life as a performance'. Like so many performers with inordinately high opinions of themselves, refusing to leave the stage is less a choice than an addiction. Lest we forget, Johnson was born in the USA and one of the historic characters from his birthplace that he echoes is that of the snake oil salesman, toxic dissemblers both. He's doubtless mindful, too, of that famous Americanism 'It ain't over till the fat lady sings'.

Boris and his resurrection

Before Alexander Boris de Pfeffel Johnson had left No 10, moves already began to resurrect him from the political graveyard. Thousands of Tory supporters signed petitions to try and force his name onto the leadership ballot paper, with even an improbable legal bid to back it proposed by former Conservative party chairman and Boris cheerleader Lord Cruddas, supported by a number of former MPs and MEPs. The same Lord Cruddas confided that over lunch Boris said he still believes he could be back to lead the Tories into the next general election. Whether or not this is true is irrelevant in the Johnson universe: what matters is that it keeps his name and the possibility of a return to power in the forefront of public consciousness.

Highly improbable, but totally mission impossible? The Johnson premiership, its rise, fall, and disgrace has been like no other in modern British political history. But like him or loathe him (and I fall firmly into the latter camp) there is no denying his charisma and past ability to defy the normal rules of political gravity. To count out the possibility of him 'doing an Arnie' would be dangerous complacency, as many wise heads in both the Tory and Labour hierarchies privately acknowledge and in some cases greatly fear.

For now, however, 'Whither Boris?' is the question fascinating people well beyond the Westminster bubble, the chattering classes, and stretching across to the supermarket checkout and the saloon bar.

Musical chairs with Nadine?

Will Boris stick around as a conscientious backbench MP like the predecessor Theresa May whom he fatally knifed? Already there are signs his allies are exploring securing him a safer seat than his Uxbridge one where, which on current polling, his 7,000 majority could well see him defeated at the next general election. There are certainly whispers that his (over)devoted acolyte Nadine Dorries would accept a resignation peerage from Johnson, enabling him to stand in her Mid-Bedfordshire constituency with its near 25,000 majority. And win.

Dorries' devotion to Boris outraged even some of her allies and fellow Johnson/Truss supporters on 30 July when she retweeted a photoshopped image from a production of Shakespeare's Julius Caesar with Rishi Sunak's head replacing knife-wielding Brutus and Caesar's head replaced by Boris Johnson's. Various MPs from across the political divide angrily condemned it as 'sick and dangerous', pointing to its grotesque echoes of the knife killings of both Tory MP David Amess and Labour MP Jo Cox.

Some allies, concerned over the spectre Johnson poses to the Conservative party and its survival in power, are already working on the idea of an ego-satisfying role on the world stage that will remove him from domestic politics. One being actively mooted is succeeding Jens Stoltenberg as Nato Secretary General (salary $227,253 plus considerable perks) and plenty of prestige and opportunity to deliver Churchillian speeches.

King of the comment pages?

Will he return to his lucrative old newspaper columnist career? There are reliable sources suggesting Paul Dacre, supremo of the Mail group and stout Johnson defender, is poised to offer him a contract well in advance of the £265,000-plus a year his former (but now less loyal) home the Telegraph accorded him.

It would provide the perfect platform to wreak revenge on enemies, advise allies, deride Keir Starmer and Labour and, most of all, remind us he is convinced (like Trump, whose behaviour he now disturbingly mirrors at times, as his former boss Andrew Neil has pointedly flagged up) that he was wrongly ousted from power but remains ready and waiting in the wings.

While one former senior Johnson loyalist (now disillusioned) put it to me: 'It's been suggested to him he could emulate Tony Blair and set up a non-profit global foundation. But, with his messed-up finances, the non-profit bit wouldn't appeal. And he certainly wouldn't donate the millions from any memoirs to the British Legion as Blair did. But the millions Blair has made from the global speaker circuit and advising dirty regimes in dodgy places might well appeal. He'll also miss Chequers, the country home of the Prime Minister with its magnificent 1,500 acres, 10 bedrooms, personal chef, and large staff, rather more than No 10 with its sobering reminder of how it contributed so much to his downfall.'

Back to his birthplace?

I hear the Trump team revving up for another tilt at The White House (assuming The Donald escapes jail) believe recruiting Boris as a British voice on the campaign trail the way they did with Nigel Farage in 2020 would be a coup. Trump, of course, has previously endowed Boris with the title, the 'Britain Trump'. But this would be a courtship even he would probably be smart enough to resist consummating.

Boris could well move to the US and become a billionaire via the TV talk show and corporate speaker circuit, predicts Nigel Farage: 'Trump likes him and he gets on well with Biden, with more than a little help from Carrie, over net zero [...] despite Boris's obsession with the green agenda damaging the UK economy.'

In a hard-hitting interview with the US NBC Network, Farage, the man whose Brexit campaigning panicked the Conservative party and forced David Cameron into calling the 2016 referendum that changed Britain's history, said: 'To this day we still don't know if Boris Johnson believed in Brexit or saw it as a career opportunity, and I don't suppose we'll ever know for certain. He might have got Brexit over the line, but he hasn't got it done properly. He might have been elected as a Conservative but he governed like a Liberal. One of the messages of Brexit was to remove power from the centre but Johnson simply preserved the same old London-centric system run by the same over-privileged elite, most of whom have never had a proper job in their lives.'

Farage also lashed out at Boris remaining in office after the mass revolt by his ministers and MPs, saying: 'He should have put Dominic Raab in temporary charge and had the decency to immediately send for the removal vans and left No 10 immediately.' He added that Johnson's 'dishonest, lying behaviour' had massively damaged public trust in politics and left the Conservative party with 'such a damaged brand, it could face a catastrophic defeat at the 2024 general election'.

Boris the born-again scholar?

Although Johnson's biography of his hero Winston Churchill was widely lambasted as 'worthless retread, lacking in insight, scholarship or new material', the insight Boris Johnson clings on to is that Churchill was the Schwarzenegger of his day, rejected repeatedly only to rise again (forget that he ultimately fell again!)

Tom Bower, author of Boris Johnson The Gambler, (2020) was recently on the money when he told various US interviewers that Bojo could guarantee $3 million minimum for his memoirs, particularly if he extended them beyond grudge-settling politics to the elusive truth about his marriages, love affairs, short flings, and exactly how many children he's sired by how many women. Bower added: 'He believes, in the long term, there is a realistic chance of a political comeback […] that, in the end, there will be that Churchillian appeal to him as the only man to save the party.'

A post-Johnson warning to the Tory party came from James Forsyth, political editor of The Spectator in his 29 July Times column. Forsyth, whose wife Allegra Stratton was the unjustly sacrificed first victim of Johnson's Partygate coverup, wrote: 'His legacy for the party is complicated: he vanquished Corbynism, broke the Brexit deadlock and created a new electoral coalition. He was also responsible for his own downfall and made the positions of his colleagues untenable. If the Tories dont work out what they think of him now, the question will bedevil them, particularly as the sheer force of his personality means he won't fade into the background.'

In the immediate term Johnson, whose personal finances have always been as chaotic as his political legacy, has to produce his long-overdue biography of Shakespeare for which he allegedly received a £500,000 advance that helped pay his divorce bills while also contributing to his failure to attend the first five Covid Cabinet Office Briefing Rooms (COBRA) meetings in March 2020.

Some allies fear, while opponents fervently hope, that the long delayed (by Boris) independent public inquiry into the Covid crisis will prove the decisive fatal blow to his dreams (delusions?) of that Schwarzeneggeresque comeback to the highest office.

The one certainty now in the still unfolding Johnson story is uncertainty. As the No 10 door closes behind him, enemies and allies alike are already shaping up to write the final chapter, a melodrama guaranteed; tragi-comedy too. Shakespeare himself would have loved to script it.

References

William Hague (2022) 'Tories must beware Boris the incredible sulk', The Times, 25 July.

CURTAIN

Gina Miller on big lies, little lies, and Boris

We're sat in the main hall at the Conservative Party conference on the Business Day 9 October 2012 awaiting the next speaker, one Mr Boris Johnson, then Mayor of London. The buzz in the room was electric and filled with a mix of excitement and anticipation as if the audience were awaiting a famous actor or comedian.

From where I was sitting, I could see the side of the stage and soon saw the man himself ruffle his hair and bend down to tuck one of his trouser legs into his sock, then on to the stage he bounded. The show had begun and the audience who enabled this actor/clown exploded into rapturous applause. Mr Johnson began his speech by gazing out into the audience and saying: 'Where is Dave?' Having spotted the then prime minister, he wished him a happy birthday and backed his strategy to 'turn the country round'. This is when I first realised not only that Johnson had 'star' quality in the eyes of Tory politicians and members, but to him power was a game he would play to win, whatever the costs.

One thing that shines through the previous thirty chapters in this book is the duplicity of Boris Johnson.

A narcissist and liar who wanted to be world king from a young age, he could fool some people all of the time. As a journalist he was eventually brought down by his tissue of lies. As prime minister the same by Partygate and the breaking of lockdown rules he had himself imposed on the nation and which meant tens of thousands of people never got to say goodbye to loved ones who died alone. In his wake there is always chaos and damage to the institutions, people and fabric of the positions he has held.

Everyone tells a lie, little or big, and over a lifetime, we all tell many lies. But I have concluded that Johnson is a narcissist, a liar. It isn't just what he does, it is who he is. He doesn't have an undeveloped sense of self but a fragmented sense of self. A self-based on opportunism instead of values. In his profession and private life, it's all a game and one he plays to win.

For the Conservative Party to have allowed such a man to hold the office of Prime Minister is a dereliction of care, duty and responsibility to the people of Britain. He has stretched the 'good chap' model of government to its limits and the result is that trust in government and politicians is at rock bottom and tainted for years to come. His vanity and desire to surround himself with a cultish Cabinet has shaken the foundation of our representative democracy, allowed in people more ideologically right wing than himself to hold the reins of power, and enabled a Westminster culture where truth, honesty and integrity have been abandoned.

The Johnson era may be over, but the damage is far from over.

His lying was not news to me. I myself was caught up in his duplicity over the illegal prorogation of Parliament in 2019. He persuaded his Cabinet that this was necessary to get his government business through. 'Remainers' were supposedly conspiring to block his 'get Brexit done' strategy and his co-conspirator Jacob Rees-Mogg, then Leader of the House of Commons and the Chief Whip were sent scurrying to Balmoral to lie to the Queen.

In numerous long letters exchanged between his lawyers and mine during August 2019, I was repeatedly reassured that Parliament would not be prorogued for five weeks leading to the real possibility of Parliament being shut out of the Brexit deal process and the UK crashing out of the EU with no deal. I received the very last reassurance over the weekend of 6 September, yet on Monday morning 9 September Johnson announced he would formally suspend parliament for five weeks. We lodged our case, which I had instructed my legal team to carry on preparing, that afternoon as however much they tried to reassure me that this was not an option for Johnson, I have never trusted him.

This constitutional outrage and lying to the Queen made me very angry as the precedent it would set for future prime ministers would be unthinkable and move the UK towards being the 'elective dictatorship' warned of by Lord Hailsham. My father was a criminal barrister and then Attorney General in my native Guyana and he taught me the importance of no one being above the law, the separation of powers and the duty of the law and courts to exercise constitutional checks and balances of those misusing power. The urgency of the prorogation case, and the desire of the courts not to frustrate the Brexit political timetable meant the hearing in the highest court in the land, the Supreme Court, was swift. We won a unanimous judgment with Lady Hale, the then chair, unequivocal in her judgement 'It follows that Parliament has not been prorogued and that this court should make declarations to that effect. We have been told by counsel for the Prime Minister that he will "take all necessary steps to comply with the terms of any declaration made by the court" and we expect him to do so. However, it appears to us that, as Parliament is not prorogued, it is for Parliament to decide what to do next.'

Sitting listening to the judgment being read out was an emotional roller-coaster as it was hard to tell if we had won until the very last sentences. The liar had been defeated, I thought order would be restored – but, alas, I underestimated the damage he would do to our rights, in closing down our rights on the streets, in the courts and at the ballot box with a raft of draconian legislation – the Police and Courts Act, the Nationality and Borders Act, Courts Act, Elections Act all received royal assent on 28 April 2022.

Commentators say that the British public 'baked in' the Johnson tangential relationship to the truth in their view of 'Boris'. Hence his huge majority in the General Election in December 2019 just three months after my victory in the courts. Going around the country with my new True & Fair Party, this is true but the number of lies and callous disregard for sexual misconduct, corruption, cronyism, honesty and integrity has unleashed anger amongst the British public that I feel is underestimated by the Tory Party. In being complicit in electing Johnson as their leader and then in No 10 the Conservative Party may well have destroyed their party and respect for the office of prime minister for decades.

For my part, there is a silver lining. Johnson's stretching of the elastic of truth and the limited accountability in our naïve model of government in the UK, has exposed the weaknesses and systemic failures in our machinery of government. It is time for legislative check and balances so no Prime Minister, Executive or MP can get away with disgraceful behaviour, lying, corruption or misusing our public funds. Voters should not have to be stressed and concerned about the veracity and character of the people for whom they vote to represent them. If there is wrongdoing, there should be redress.

Politicians are expected to lie but not as a default position. Boris Johnson's credibility has disappeared, but so too has that of his party and UK political reputation – domestically and internationally. His chaotic antics have led to the UK being referred to by foreign countries as 'Carry on UK' as told to me by an ex-UK Ambassador at Desmond Tutu's Memorial service in London I was attending.

I am glad to see the back of him. It is now time to reshape and strengthen our political systems, to clean up politics, modernise our democracy and fight corruption. This is why I continue to exercise my civic duty and formed the True & Fair Party – it is time for a new type of politics, for the new realities heading towards all of us. It is time to put in laws to stop another liar to represent us.

About the contributor

Gina Miller is a social justice campaigner who defeated Johnson's government over the prorogation of parliament in 2019. She is the founder and leader of the True & Fair Party

Printed in Great Britain
by Amazon

84910741R00098